CW00840608

Shetland

Baltasound

UNST

● Uyeasound

Gutcher ●

FETLAR

*Yell
Sound*

YELL

*Colgrave
Sound*

NORTHMAVINE

● Ulsta

DELTING   **LUNNASTING**

**OUT
SKERRIES**

St Magnus Bay

● Brae

Vidlin ●

WHALSAY

**PAPA
STOUR**

Dury Voe ● Symbister

NESTING

**WEST
MAINLAND**

● Aith

South Nesting Bay

**CENTRAL
MAINLAND**

Walls ●

BRESSAY

Lerwick ●

FOULA

NOSS

Scalloway

**SOUTH
MAINLAND**

Sumburgh

FAIR ISLE

Food Made in Shetland

Food
Made in
Shetland

Marian Armitage

60 North
Publishing

60 North Publishing
7 Mounthooly Street, Lerwick, Shetland ZE1 0BJ
www.60northpublishing.com

First published in Great Britain in 2022 by 60 North Publishing.

A catalogue record for this book is available from the British Library.

ISBN 978-1-80068-813-1

Publishing and Creative Director: Misa Hay
Photographer: Susan Molloy
Artwork: Gilly Bridle
Design: Left Design

Printed and bound in the Czech Republic.
For more information visit www.60northpublishing.com

Dedicated with love,
to the memory of
Wilma Young

Contents

he beautiful south end of Shetland, da Ness, is where my father's family came from. Scatness is the fascinating peninsula of land that points southwards, between Sumburgh Head and Fitful Head with Fair Isle on the horizon, and witnesses the most extreme variations of Shetland weather.

The fierce south-westerly gales which lash the black cliffs send waves and spindrift high into the air and then right across this bleak headland.

A walk to the ancient blockhouse at the end of the Ness of Burgi fills me with awe and wonder at who might have lived there and how they survived. There are regular sightings of seals throughout the year, the most breathtaking carpet of sea-pinks in May and mirror-calm rock pools for swimming in fine weather. You can see ancient boat noosts where the traditional Ness yoals were pulled well clear of the sea, and over a dozen remains of plantiecrubs in which the local folk used to grow vegetables – particularly their kale plants.

In mid-summer, including the dazzling sunrise behind Sumburgh Head, and the spectacular sunset over Fitful, there are 22 hours of daylight in the 'simmer dim'. In winter the mirrie dancers (aurora borealis) light the sky and the reassuring three-flash signal from the Sumburgh Head lighthouse sweeps through the house every 30 seconds.

Within the horizon, fishing boats, the *Good Shepherd* on her voyage to Fair Isle, the NorthLink ferry, cruise ships and sailing boats of all sizes have to face the challenge of the Sumburgh Roost – the pull of the strong tidal stream which goes round this most southerly tip of the Shetland Mainland.

This is my kitchen panorama and where all the recipes in this book were made for Susan Molloy's beautiful and creative photography.

All of my life I have enjoyed food and cooking. I was inspired by excellent teaching at the Anderson High School in Lerwick, then four years being taught Domestic Science at what is now Queen Margaret University in Edinburgh. This was followed by a 35-year career teaching Food and Nutrition to 12-19 year olds, and during that time my love of food has not ever diminished.

I wrote *Shetland Food and Cooking* in 2014, not long after retiring. It includes background about Shetland agriculture, fishing and crofting life together with many traditional and contemporary recipes highlighting the wonderful produce that we have here in Shetland. The book was shortlisted for the Gourmand World Cookbook Awards – a four-day event in Yantai, China, in May 2016, where it was the winner in the Food Promotion category. A truly unforgettable event.

This book came about through my work in recent years with Misa Hay. Cooking for participants on her Shetland Wool Adventures tours provided an opportunity to present delicious Shetland food to an interested audience in a convivial setting.

Another book was not planned but Covid-19 lockdowns provided time to think and reflect, and I realised that I very much wanted to continue to share my knowledge and experience. I feel great pride in the food we produce and I am always curious and enjoy experimenting with ideas. Showing people how to create dishes and meals, together with providing encouragement as skills develop and improve, is what I really believe in and find enormously rewarding, especially as I now have three grandchildren.

I have enjoyed having many opportunities too, to work with bairns in primary and secondary schools in Shetland, watching their eagerness and enthusiasm and challenging their tastebuds while showing them new ideas with local food.

Shetland is now a celebrated travel destination. Exposure through good travel journalism, the work of Promote Shetland and television series – including the Shetland crime drama, Island Medics and wildlife and farming programmes – as well as many visitors on cruise ships and to Shetland Wool Week have all contributed.

We have world-class food produced, caught, reared and grown here and although we don't have Michelin-starred restaurants we have creative, ingenious cooks, with enthusiasm and passion for sharing the local produce.

I want to encourage and inspire you to be creative with our local food. Shetland is a unique place and the food is too.

Fruit & Vegetables

There are few things more rewarding, in my view, than growing vegetables. From sowing seeds to nurturing the plant and then cooking and eating it. Last summer was the best year ever for my outdoor parsley – it was bushy and about a foot high. It tasted great and features frequently in these photos!

There has been a significant increase in folk growing their own fruit and vegetables in Shetland – but also a greater awareness of Shetland's vulnerability as weather and climate increasingly affect normal food supply.

Using a polytunnel provides a little more shelter for the grower and the Shetland-developed Polycrub (polycrub.co.uk), cleverly designed and using recycled materials from the salmon farming industry, has been a huge success with over 460 in use in Shetland, and over 1,100 across the UK.

They can increase the growing season by up to 100 days and it is estimated that they can produce over 30kg of food per year. They are increasingly popular for educational and therapeutic purposes too with community groups, schools, care homes and also the Hillswick GP surgery patients' group.

A huge range of plants can be grown or at least started off in a polycrub and a photo of a 10½ lbs crop of lemons was recently posted on social media. There is still some way to go before Shetland can be self-sufficient in fruit and vegetables, but the gap can be closed with cleverly planned gardening.

This is definitely a goal that Penny Armstrong and Alan Robertson at Transition Turriefield have had since 2008 when they first started experimenting, and growing what is now a huge range of vegetables. They are a not-for-profit community interest company and the largest business growing and selling organic produce within Shetland. They rely on help from volunteers and sell their produce mainly through a vegbox scheme with surplus going to local shops.

They were recently awarded funding from the Coastal Communities' Fund to establish 'Grow Shetland' – a three-year project to support the Shetland community to grow more of its own fruit and vegetables, increase skills and improve access to affordable food and encourage healthy eating. They run workshops and classes and also link experienced growers with novices in order to share knowledge, and act as mentors.

Throughout Shetland there are an increasing number of growers offering vegboxes and local shops and honesty boxes sell surplus when available.

Growing vegetables has always been a significant part of crofting life and traditional root vegetables remain the staples in an outdoor Shetland garden: taaties – including the famous Shetland Black; neeps (swede) and carrots together with Shetland kale (*Brassica oleracea L*). Rhubarb and gooseberries also grow in abundance.

The Mackenzie family at Aister in Cunningsburgh and Grow Local Northmavine are now selling genuine Shetland kale seed commercially and many growers save and share their own seed.

For a number of years now I have been fortunate to receive peerie kale plants from veteran Shetland gardener and writer Barbara Fraser's self-built plantiecrub – she saves her own seed and grows plants on every year before transplanting them to her kale-yard. A plantiecrub is a traditional stone shelter – either round or square, to protect young plants from sheep as well as the elements. Barbara's splendid new book *Aye someen deid, aye someen boarn*, in Shetland dialect, is available from the Shetland Times Bookshop and includes stories from her crofting life.

There are, however, many many experienced and creative Shetland growers, all over the isles, and a conversation with any of them, whose wisdom about the weather, pests, best varieties to choose as well as the nuances of cultivation, is more valuable than any book or internet search.

Spinach Soup with Nutmeg

The colour of this soup is amazing and the flavour truly lovely. It is also incredibly nutritious: protein and calcium in the milk and iron in the spinach. It is best made using freshly grown leaf spinach from your garden or Polycrub (Shetland-made polytunnel), however, it can be made successfully with bagged baby spinach or frozen leaf spinach. It is really quick to make, but don't overcook the spinach.

Serves 4

400g fresh spinach – rinsed in cold water

1 medium-sized onion – roughly chopped

1 clove garlic – crushed and chopped

25g butter or 2 tablespoons oil (for cooking onion/garlic)

25g plain flour

25g butter (for the sauce)

500ml milk

350ml vegetable stock

Nutmeg – freshly grated

1 Make a thin white sauce: melt the butter, stir in the flour, cook slowly for 2 minutes, add milk and whisk well. Set aside. (This could be done in advance.)

2 If you are using fresh leaf spinach, tear away any thick stems and wash the leaves well in cold water. Set aside.

3 In a large pan, melt the butter and slowly sauté the onion and garlic till soft – a good 5-7 minutes.

4 Add the spinach and allow to wilt – this will only need a very few minutes.

5 Add the white sauce and stock to the spinach pan and mix well.

6 Pureé with a stick blender until smooth, taste, and add pepper and a little salt if necessary.

7 Serve with freshly grated nutmeg over the top.

This soup goes particularly well with warm Cheese and Thyme Scones (see page 50).

Beetroot Hummus

Beetroot is a popular vegetable to grow in Shetland and, although many folk like them pickled, there are endless creative ways to use them. Keen beetroot growers can also grow yellow (or golden) as well as pink and white striped varieties which look tremendous in a salad or roasted as an accompaniment to a main dish. I have used an extremely purple variety for this recipe. Hummus really is so very easy to make – and it freezes perfectly in peerie (small) pots.

Serves 6
as a starter or snack

1 x 400g can chick peas in water (reserve 3 or 4 chickpeas to garnish)

3 tablespoons tahini (sesame seed paste)

1 tablespoon olive oil

2 cloves garlic – crushed and finely chopped

1 rounded teaspoon ground cumin (for an enhanced flavour use whole cumin seeds, warm slightly then grind in a pestle and mortar)

2 medium-sized beetroots – cooked (boil or roast) and cut roughly into cubes (keep 2 or 3 thin slices back for decoration)

½ level teaspoon salt

Freshly ground pepper

Beetroot hummus – with a touch of ground cumin looks and tastes delicious and beautiful – but don't stop at beetroot. Try roast carrot and coriander hummus or spinach hummus for a colourful collection of starters.

In addition to using as a dip with vegetable crudités (fennel, peppers, celery, carrots etc) or pitta bread, these 'hummusses' are delicious on open sandwiches, in wraps and as part of a sharing platter.

If there is a vegan in your life, remember to save the water (from the tinned chick peas) – or aquafaba – which can be whisked successfully to replicate some of the functions of egg white, for example, in meringue.

1   Using a stick blender mix everything thoroughly. Add a little warm water if it is too thick.

2   Transfer to a shallow serving dish and garnish with sliced beetroot and chick peas – optional. That's it!

Spiced Carrot Chutney

Here is another great recipe using the splendid carrots that grow in Shetland, particularly in the sandy soil in and around the Ness. Thank you to Deepa, my daughter-in-law, for inspiration with this recipe. The combinations of flavours here are so great; they won't blast your head off but you will want to go back for at least another spoonful. It would be best to make this on a fine day with the windows open!

Makes 6 medium-sized jars

1 kg carrots – grated

60g fresh ginger

4 red chillis – de-seeded and finely chopped

20g coriander seeds

2 x 10cm cinnamon sticks

2 star anise

30g salt

500ml cider vinegar

10g cumin seeds

10 cardamom pods – deseeded

16 cloves garlic – crushed and finely chopped

200ml water

350g granulated sugar

Day 1

Preparation. In a large, stainless steel pan mix together the carrots, ginger, chillis, spices, salt and cider vinegar.

Leave to marinade for 24 hours.

Day 2

Add garlic, water and sugar – bring to a rolling boil for 10 minutes then lower the heat and simmer till reduced and thickened (approx 2-3 hours).

Allow to cool before potting into sterilised jars.

This chutney will keep well for at least 6 months.

● This goes particularly well with the Shetland Hand-raised Pork Pie (see page 128).

Salsa Verde

This is the most useful of sauces and can be varied according to the basic herbs you have available, as well as to its end use. It is sharp and vinegary, full of fresh herb flavours and very versatile. Think of a basic vinaigrette salad dressing with the addition of lots of fresh chopped herbs. I like to add capers and gherkins – a favourite in fish dishes – and many folk add anchovy, too, to add another layer of flavour.

Makes 1 jar

2 cloves garlic

2 handfuls parsley

1 small bunch basil

1 handful mint

1 tablespoon capers

2-3 gherkins

2 teaspoons Dijon mustard

3 tablespoons vinegar
– red or white

8 tablespoons olive oil

Freshly ground black pepper

1 level teaspoon salt

You can use this as a marinade or add to a tablespoonful of yogurt as a dip. It can accompany grilled or roast meat – particularly beef or lamb, or oily fish such as herring, mackerel or salmon. It is good with roast vegetables and is great spread on a wrap before adding a filling of your choice.

Last year, I had such success growing curly parsley, it was lovely and thick and about a foot high! Chives, too, grew really well so I made plenty of this sauce. It will keep well in a clean jar in the fridge for at least two weeks.

Add all ingredients to a food processor and whizz together. Alternatively, pulverise using a stick blender in a deep container, or use a pestle and mortar.

That's it!

Fresh Orange Conserve

Every January, my kitchen – and often the whole house – is full of the aromas of marmalade making, as the Seville oranges are in season. It's just one of those traditions for me and I've always used the same recipe and always involved the bairns for help. Sometimes we run out before the next season. Toast without home made marmalade? Na na! So, here is a delicious recipe that can be made 12 months a year!

Makes 4-6 medium-sized jars

2 large oranges (approx 600g)

1 lemon – finely grated rind and juice

1 litre water

450g granulated sugar

1 Wash the fruit in warm water.

2 Slice the whole oranges thinly then cut each slice into small wedge shaped pieces, saving all the juice as you go. Discard all the pips. This is a slow process – a shared job, ideally.

3 Place all the prepared orange together with the lemon rind and juice and the water into a large pan.

4 Bring to the boil then cook slowly, over a very low heat, for approximately 2 hours.

5 Wash and sterilise 4-6 jars by placing them in the oven at 100°C.

6 If possible, warm the sugar in a low oven: 100°C for 15 minutes.

7 Place three saucers into the fridge (for testing the set).

8 Switch off the heat and add the sugar slowly, stirring gently till it dissolves.

9 Now raise the heat till you have a rolling boil. Boil for approximately 15 minutes then test for a set by placing a spoonful of the mixture on to a cold saucer and watching for the surface to crinkle.

10 It may be necessary to repeat this crinkle test twice more at 3-minute intervals.

11 When set, allow to cool slightly then fill the jars and finish as you wish with wax or wax discs etc.

➲ Thank you to Marthe Armitage, my mother-in-law, for this super recipe.
Apart from this lovely fruity jam, she also creates beautiful wallpapers and fabrics.
www.marthearmitageprints.com

FRESH ORANGE
CONSERVE

FRESH ORANGE
CONSERVE

FRESH ORANGE
CONSERVE

Rhubarb Cordial

This cordial is a lovely summer drink and looks so pretty, too. It is also good to be able to offer something other than fruit juice to children and those not drinking alcohol. I have been experimenting with proportions and think I have achieved a balance between not being 'ower shilpit' (too sharp) whilst reducing sugar levels to an acceptable proportion.

Makes 500ml

500g rhubarb

500ml cold water

100g granulated sugar

Another delightful rhubarb drink – this time sparkling – is created in one of the Taste of Shetland short films (**www.tasteofshetland.com**). Demonstrated by Mary Andreas, treasurer of Shetland Food and Drink and proprietor of the 4 star B&B – Hayhoull. It can't be called champagne, as it was made in Bigton!

1 Wipe the stalks of the rhubarb and cut roughly into 1cm pieces.

2 Add the cold water and bring to the boil. Simmer for about 20 minutes until totally mushy. Then stir in the sugar, allow to dissolve, and simmer for a further 5 minutes.

3 Strain the mixture through a sieve and allow to cool. This will produce about 500ml and should be diluted 50:50 with sparkling or still water.

4 Why not experiment by adding mint leaves, slices of orange, cucumber, strawberry – Pimms-style – for a really exotic party drink?

For even more recipes check out the fascinating book, *Rhubarbaria*, by Mary Prior.

Rhubarb Compôte

Rhubarb grows abundantly in Shetland. It is officially a vegetable but is certainly treated as a fruit by the many Shetlanders who create a huge variety of dishes from this plant that simply appears year after year without fail. When I was peerie (small), at school and at home stewed rhubarb was a fairly standard pudding – usually with custard but also (shudder) with semolina or tapioca – and I do remember it getting very green and stringy as the season progressed. In *Shetland Food and Cooking* there are five good rhubarb recipes: for a cake, an interesting jam, a fruity chutney, a stuffing for mackerel and a very alcoholic hooch. Here is my basic cooking method where the rhubarb barely sees water.

Serves 4

500g rhubarb

40g granulated sugar

1 tablespoon of water

1 Preheat the oven to 180°C.

2 Wipe the stalks with a damp cloth and cut into pieces 2-3cm – and at an angle to look attractive.

3 Spread out on a flat ovenproof dish – glass, china or enamel are best.

4 Sprinkle the sugar over and add a tablespoon of water.

5 Bake, uncovered, for about 25 minutes; turn gently halfway through cooking using a fish slice.

6 The sugar will draw moisture from the rhubarb and you will end up with full-flavoured fruit that keeps its shape. Set aside; it will continue cooking as it cools.

7 You can now use it in a cake, crumble, pie or with ice-cream or yoghurt and maybe add some of the other flavours that go well with rhubarb – orange, strawberry, ginger, cinnamon and star anise are among my favourites. You can also freeze it, ready for use at another time.

Roast Carrot Salad

Together with taaties and neeps (known as swede to many) carrots are one of the most traditional Shetland vegetables and they will keep through the winter till early spring ideally stored in sand in a frost free shed. Here is a great way of using carrots if you have had enough of them raw and grated. The toasted pumpkin seeds add a good crunch to the texture. The addition of a very small quantity of oil and seasonings before roasting really enhances the natural sweetness – I hope you will try this combination of flavours and experiment with other variations.

Serves 4-6, depending on how many other dishes are on offer

500g carrots

1 tablespoon rapeseed oil

Large pinch salt

Freshly ground black pepper

1 teaspoon dried oregano or thyme

4 spring onions – finely sliced

1 red skinned apple – finely diced, skin on

1 tablespoon pumpkin seeds – lightly toasted

Big handful fresh coriander – roughly chopped

Vinaigrette

3 tablespoons olive oil

1 tablespoon balsamic vinegar

1 teaspoon grain mustard

1 finely chopped clove garlic

1   Preheat the oven to 220°C.

2   Put the oil, salt, pepper and dried herbs into a large mixing bowl.

3   Cut the carrots into even-sized sticks and toss well until they are lightly coated.

4   Transfer to a baking sheet and spread out roughly.

5   Roast near the top of the oven for about 20-25 minutes, turning half-way through with a fish slice. Allow to cool.

6   Prepare the apple, spring onion and coriander and mix with the vinaigrette ingredients.

7   Add the carrots and serve garnished with the toasted pumpkin seeds.

➲ This is a great salad for a party alongside other vegetable dishes – and it is totally plant-based.

Shetland Kale and Tomato Salad with Hazelnuts

This simple dish uses lightly steamed kale. Shetland kale is very attractive indeed, with rich dark green leaves and purple ribs. While it is usually just simply steamed or boiled, this combination is a real change from the traditional way of cooking this Shetland staple. Curly kale and cavolo nero would be equally suitable if you are far away from 'da kale yard'. Using hazelnut oil and crunchy toasted hazelnuts produces a really lovely contrast of flavours and textures. You can make this several hours in advance – just keep it covered in a cool place.

Serves 4

Shetland kale – 8 medium-sized leaves, well rinsed

12 peerie (small) cherry tomatoes – halved

3 tablespoons hazelnut oil (use olive oil if this is not available)

1 tablespoon wine vinegar

25g toasted hazelnuts – roughly chopped

1   Finely shred the kale and steam for approximately 5-8 minutes until just done.

2   Tip into a bowl and add the halved tomatoes, oil and vinegar, a pinch of salt and a good grind of black pepper. The warmth of the kale will help all the ingredients to amalgamate.

3   Just before serving, sprinkle the hazelnuts over.

⊙ Kale is so incredibly nutritious; it is rich in vitamin A, which is needed for the maintenance of normal vision, and also for a healthy immune system.

With two grandchildren who are half Australian, and having made a couple of longer visits to Australia, I have been inspired by Aussie cooking and baking to make more use of all kinds of nuts with all those healthy anti-oxidants. If you toast them first – they become more crunchy and the flavours are better.

Root Vegetable Upside Down Tart
with Goat Cheese and Walnut Pastry

This is a great vegetarian recipe which I have made on several occasions for guests on 'Shetland Wool Adventures' dinners. The principle of a tarte tatin, where fruit – usually apples – is cooked underneath the pastry then served upside down is just superb as there is no soggy-bottom danger and advanced pastry skills are not required as the crust is not on view. Consequently, it is an ideal dish to make, sweet or savoury, when teaching beginners. This recipe has walnuts in the pastry, giving terrific flavours, extra nutrients and a lovely crispness. You could also make this as a starter, cut into small slices, or take it on a picnic – tin and all.

Serves 6-8

Pastry

150g plain flour

75g butter

50g roughly chopped walnuts

6 teaspoons cold water

Salt and freshly ground pepper

Filling

100g goat cheese (I like to use the small round log, for ease of cutting)

150g parsnips

150g carrots

150g neep (swede)

Chives for garnish

1 Have ready a 23cm sandwich tin.

2 Prepare the vegetables and cut into chunks or slices. Part-cook by steaming for 10 minutes. Allow to cool.

3 Make the pastry: rub the butter into the flour, add walnuts, salt and pepper then the water. Mix well.

4 Knead lightly and roll out to form a circle to fit. Place on a sheet of baking paper and chill in the fridge while you make the filling.

5 Preheat the oven to 190°C.

6 Layer the vegetables with thin slices of the goat cheese. Season well.

7 Place the pastry over the top and press firmly.

8 Bake for 40-50 minutes. Allow to cool slightly then upturn on to a serving platter.

9 Garnish with finely chopped chives and some more chopped walnuts.

➲ As always, you can vary the ingredients. By substituting the dairy produce for plant-based alternatives, this makes a superb vegan main course.

Roast Crunchy Cauliflower with Cauliflower Purée

The range of vegetables grown in Shetland has been increasing over the last few years and several growers now offer veg boxes on a regular basis for periods of the year. Whilst the classic cauliflower cheese is a firm family favourite, I have been experimenting with ways to try and celebrate the delicate flavour of this vegetable. Cauliflower is definitely best steamed, rather than boiled, and broken into smaller florets, but do try this recipe which gives different textures: a creamy cauliflower purée in a béchamel sauce contrasting with the nicely charred, crunchy roast slices, sprinkled with toasted flaked almonds.

Serves 6

2 medium-sized cauliflowers – outer leaves removed

2 tablespoons olive oil

1 teaspoon salt

Freshly ground pepper

300ml full fat milk

1 rounded teaspoon plain flour

25g butter

1 bay leaf

2 slices onion

1 tablespoon flaked almonds – toasted in a dry pan for 5 minutes

2 finely sliced spring onions

I have given the recipe for a classic béchamel just because the flavour is so delicate and complementary to the cauliflower. If you are in a hurry, omit the infusing of the milk. By substituting the dairy ingredients with suitable alternatives, this recipe would be perfect as the basis of a main course for someone following a vegan diet.

1   Put the milk, onion and bay leaf into a small pan over a medium heat. When the milk is hot, but not boiling, switch off the heat and leave to infuse for at least half an hour. Alternatively, make the sauce the day before.

2   Preheat the oven to 220°C.

3   Cut 6 x 1-2cm thick slices right through the cauliflowers. In a shallow dish – and with your hands – rub oil, salt and pepper well into both sides.

4   Place on a baking tray near the top of the oven and roast for 15-20 minutes, turning once half-way through. The aim is to have nicely browned and slightly charred edges.

5   Strain the infused milk into a jug. Rinse out the pan and make a basic roux sauce by melting the butter, stirring in the flour, and cooking for 2-3 moments over a low heat before adding the warm milk gradually and whisking thoroughly. Cook over a low heat for 5 minutes.

6   Meanwhile, steam the remaining parts of the cauliflowers, which are likely to be in bruck (fallen apart), for approximately 5 minutes.

7   When just done, purée coarsely with a stick blender and add to the sauce.

8   Mix thoroughly and taste, adding salt and pepper as required.

9   Arrange on a serving dish or straight on to warmed plates and garnish with toasted flaked almonds and thinly sliced spring onion.

Le Poirat
Pear Tart with Walnut and Cinnamon Pastry

This tart has such a lovely combination of flavours and textures. It is straightforward, French inspired, and is one that I made in my student days at the Edinburgh College of Domestic Science – as it then was – in the early 1970s. I'm really keen on using nuts as an ingredient as the cooking process enhances the flavour and improves the texture. This is not a showy dessert, but crisp fragrant pastry, soft juicy pears and a light cloud of fresh cream – delicious.

Serves 4-6

200g plain flour

125g unsalted butter

A pinch of salt

2 level teaspoons ground cinnamon

50g walnuts roughly chopped

25g caster sugar

1 egg

6 medium – similar
sized – firm pears

1 tablespoon granulated sugar

5cm piece cinnamon stick

Whipped cream to serve

1 First make the pastry: rub the butter into the flour, with a pinch of salt and the ground cinnamon and sugar, until the mixture resembles fine crumbs.

2 Stir in the walnuts.

3 Add the beaten egg and about a teaspoon of cold water; stir well till the mixture all comes together.

4 Knead gently on a lightly floured surface, then cover and refrigerate while you prepare the pears.

5 Dissolve a tablespoon of granulated sugar in about 250ml water and bring to the boil; simmer for 2-3 minutes. Add the cinnamon stick.

6 Peel, quarter and core the pears and poach gently in the sugar syrup for about 5 minutes. Switch off the heat and allow to stand.

7 Preheat the oven to 200°C.

8 Now the pastry. Cut about a third off and set aside for the lid.

9 Roll out the remainder and line a 20cm loose-bottomed tin or flan ring.

10 Roll out a circle to fit as a lid, and cut a 6cm diameter hole in the centre.

11 Arrange the pears beautifully with the pointed end towards the centre.

12 Fit the lid and crimp the edge; press to make a neat join.

13 Brush with water and dust with caster sugar.

14 Bake for 30-40 minutes – reduce the heat to 150°C after 20 minutes.

15 Serve warm or cold. Just before serving, spoon the whipped cream into the centre of the tart.

Eggs & Dairy

Shetland Farm Dairies is a small and very-important-to-Shetland business with just two farms supplying fresh milk daily for sale throughout the isles. In addition to the usual three grades of milk sold in cartons, there are five refill stations in a number of locations around Shetland where customers can buy milk in their re-usable glass bottles with no plastic involved. The roll-out of these was halted because of Covid-19 regulations but the dairy is ready to expand with these as soon the time is right.

The dairy also makes lightly salted butter (and unsalted to order) and three grades of cream and buttermilk. It enjoys a loyal clientele in the face of direct competition from supermarkets whose milk is sold as a loss leader.

Those of us who passionately support the dairy find it hard to countenance buying milk which has had to travel north from the Scottish mainland when a truly excellent product is on our doorstep. When the ferries are disrupted due to bad weather, and supermarket shelves are empty, there is still plenty of local milk to go round. Buttermilk is the slightly acidic liquid that remains after butter is made and it is widely used in Shetland – particularly for making bannocks where it reacts with baking soda to produce carbon dioxide to make a mixture rise. It is wonderful to watch this in just two or three minutes when, for example, cooking girdle bannocks. Do try the delicious buttermilk ice cream in this chapter too.

Many Shetlanders will remember with affection the consumption of 'kirn milk' which is a light, crumbly soft cheese made from the further churning of buttermilk. Very few people still make this but it has been captured in a lovely short film at **www.tasteofshetland.com** film, as part of the heritage series.

There is no commercial production of cheese in Shetland at the moment, nor yoghurt, but Island Larder make an absolutely delicious gelato-type ice cream using Shetland milk and cream.

The recipe was specially designed to suit the characteristics of the milk by an expert ice cream technician who worked with the business. It is sold in their super Lerwick shop in a range of 12 flavours at a time, with delicious sorbets too.

Eggs are another staple and they are available all over Shetland, including in Lerwick, in roadside honesty boxes as well in local independent shops. The yolks of these eggs are such a deep yellow and the taste is superb. Usually it's hens' eggs but often duck eggs too. Scoop Wholefoods in Lerwick sell quail and guinea fowl eggs from crofts on the beautiful Lunna peninsula.

There are a number of businesses producing free range eggs on a larger scale in both Bressay and Whalsay, with a more recent venture in the North Mainland where opaque polycrubs (which regulate heat more efficiently) are used as rather up-market 'hen-hooses' hence the name 'Hensington Palace'. They also have breeds of hens some of which produce the most beautifully coloured eggs: blue, green, brown and white – with stunning deep yellow/orange yolks.

We are really fortunate to have these key ingredients with fantastic provenance on our doorstep, enabling quick meals and snacks to be rustled up as well as providing the mainstay of wonderful Shetland baking.

Spinach and Cheese Soufflé

Do not be faird (afraid) to try this – it really is not difficult. It looks lovely either in a larger dish or in peerie (small) ramekins. It can be prepared in advance – up to the folding in of egg whites stage. It makes a good vegetarian main course or a lighter starter for a bigger dinner.

Serves 4

25g butter

25g plain flour

150ml milk

Ground black pepper

½ teaspoon Dijon mustard

Freshly grated nutmeg

75g strong hard cheese – grated (Gruyère or cheddar are good)

3 eggs – separated

125g bag of spinach (freshly grown leaf spinach would be better) – cooked, well drained and chopped

1   Preheat the oven to 190°C.

2   Grease the soufflé dish or ramekins.

3   Put milk, butter and flour into a small pan and whisk or beat constantly till you have a very thick white sauce (this is sometimes called a panada and is used when making rissoles to bind ingredients together).

4   Add seasonings.

5   Cool slightly and then add the cheese.

6   Stir in the spinach and egg yolks and mix – a spatula does the job very well.

7   You can set the mixture aside at this stage and finish the dish later.

8   Whisk the egg whites until stiff. Stir 2 tablespoons into the mixture to slacken it a little then carefully fold in the remainder with a metal tablespoon. The mixture will be thick and soft.

9   Pour into the dish(es) and place on a metal baking tray near the top of the oven.

10 Bake for 15 minutes for individual ramekins or 30 minutes for a larger dish.

11 When done, it will be risen and golden while still soft and a bit wobbly in the centre.

12 Eat straight away – maybe with a salad and crusty bread and butter.

Buttermilk Ice Cream

This recipe proudly flies the flag for our dairy – Shetland Farm Dairies –
which is a small operation with just two dairy farms supplying milk through
the year. I am the fortunate owner of an ice cream machine which makes
recipes like this really easy and quick. I have tested this recipe many times
to try and optimise the proportions and have found it needs the whole
carton of SFD buttermilk and a whole carton of SFD cream. No waste.

Serves 4

550ml Shetland Farm
Dairies buttermilk

250ml Shetland Farm
Dairies double cream

100g caster sugar

1 teaspoon vanilla essence

The sharpness of the buttermilk gives it an almost lemony flavour and
the cream keeps it rich enough. I think 100g sugar is just right as it is
likely to be accompanying something sweet. If buttermilk is difficult to
find, you can substitute plain low-fat yogurt.

This recipe does not have a cooked base so it should be consumed
within about two weeks. 'Nae faer o' dat in wiroos'! (No fear of that in
our house!)

1   Mix everything into a large jug and pour into the machine. Churn
    for about 30 minutes. The texture will be light and soft. Transfer to
    a shallow container and freeze. It is especially delicious eaten soon
    after it is made.

2   Otherwise, allow half an hour in the fridge to soften slightly
    before serving.

3   This ice cream goes really well with poached fruit – rhubarb or
    gooseberries – as well as the frangipane dessert.

Rainbow Pancakes

Making pancakes in our family started with a gift of an Icelandic pancake pan from my brother in law Hafsteinn Traustason – for he is the pancake expert in their family. When our bairns were peerie and our Icelandic family came to visit – pancakes were produced and devoured by the dozen. The pan itself is incredibly simple – it is very flat and made from really heavy aluminium. As our bairns each flew the nest for university – they were given their own as a present from Hafsteinn and Wilma – so in Bristol, Nottingham and Cardiff housefuls of students were able to enjoy this simple delight and make it their own.

Makes approximately 10

100g plain flour (sieved)

Pinch of salt

2 eggs

300ml milk

100g spinach – cooked

2 teaspoons turmeric

1 medium cooked beetroot

1 Put the flour and salt into a large jug or mixing bowl.

2 Add the eggs and mix using a hand whisk.

3 Add the milk gradually until the batter is smooth.

4 Divide into smaller bowls according to your preferred colour scheme.

5 Now for the food colouring!

For green: make about 2 tablespoons spinach pureé – cook fresh or frozen spinach and then use a stick blender to achieve a smooth consistency as you add it to the batter.

For yellow: add 2 teaspoons turmeric to a portion of the plain batter and mix well.

For red/purple: pureé one cooked beetroot and add to some of the batter.

We tried to achieve a blue option by using cooked red cabbage but the taste wasn't that good! However, using red cabbage as a pH indicator provides a great opportunity for childrens' play-chemistry experiments using bicarbonate of soda and lemon juice to test. (**www.science-sparks.com**)

Perhaps your eight-year-olds can think of other possibilities?

The really fun part is cooking them and creating pretty designs then, of course, eating them with all sorts of savoury fillings: grated cheese, roast vegetables, cold ham, flaked fish, salad.

Fast forward many years and Alexander, Deepa and Ayanda have moved to Shetland. Immersed in the wonderful Bigton community there is now the Friday after school pancake club which meets in the Bigton Hall in the spring/summer/early autumn. For a nominal fee – and the rule that everyone has to have a savoury one first – vast quantities are consumed with cheese, jam, lemon, etc, then everything is packed up and bairns and parents all head down to the most famous beach in Shetland to play rounders.

In recent years I have made a number of trips to Iceland and was shocked to discover that this famous pan now costs over £60 new. However, in Reykjavik there is an amazing charity shop called the Góði hirðirinn which is translated as the Good Shepherd. There they can be bought for about £10. How satisfying.

What interesting language connections there are to Shetland too. The Good Shepherd is the name of the lifeline ferry to Fair Isle – a place that is very special for me – and, in Shetland dialect, the first line of the 23rd Psalm is: "Da Loard's my hird, I wanna want," (see **www.omaghmethodist.com** and search for Da Loard's my Hird for a full and poignant translation).

Back to the pancakes – Ayanda proudly invented these colourful variations, which took a while to perfect but created a really enjoyable Saturday morning's edible activity. Basically, you make a batch of normal pancake batter using multiples of the proportions. Thank you, Ayanda!

Marzipan and Dark Chocolate Peerie Fours

I absolutely love marzipan. My Christmas cake always has a thick layer of it under the royal icing, and this easy idea for marzipan dipped in dark chocolate, for me, is pure heaven. This recipe has a high proportion of ground almonds which makes it quite gritty and it is really, really easy to make, so try it; you'll never buy the additive-laden shop-bought stuff again. It is best made a day before use. Thank you to James for his patience and creativity.

Makes approximately 24

200g ground almonds

100g sieved icing sugar

75g caster sugar

1 egg – lightly beaten

5 drops almond essence

1 tablespoon brandy

1 tablespoon lemon juice

150g dark chocolate – for dipping

Toasted flaked almonds to decorate

1   Weigh the ground almonds and sugars into a mixing bowl.

2   Make a well in the centre and add the almond essence, brandy, lemon juice and egg.

3   Mix well with a small palette knife and then your hand, until the mixture comes together and forms a ball.

4   Wrap in baking paper and allow to chill overnight before use.

5   Roll out to about 1cm thick using a rolling pin and a little sieved icing sugar.

6   Cut out small circles or other neat shapes.

7   Melt the chocolate slowly in a bowl over hot water.

8   Now, get creative and use the chocolate, marzipan pieces and toasted almonds to create your own artisan peerie fours.

⊙ **Other uses for this delicious sweetmeat are:**

Medjool dates – stuffed with a small piece of marzipan then rolled in caster sugar.

Marzipan fruits – pieces of marzipan shaped like bananas, oranges etc.

Easter simnel cake, stollen and a delicious cake with a combination of rhubarb and marzipan from *Shetland Food and Cooking*.

Cheese and Thyme Scones

Cheese scones are just so very useful and really fast to make. Soup and twartree (two or three) of these, warm from the oven on a chilly day, is hard to beat. I used a 1½ inch (4cm) cutter; you will get at least 12 peerie scones and they will cook fast and have a good crunch on the outside. Don't roll them too thin, either – in fact, you can just use the back of your hand if you prefer. A pre-heated hot oven is essential. They will freeze well but warm them slightly before serving.

Makes approximately 15

200g self-raising flour

1 level teaspoon baking powder

25g butter

100g cheese – good strong cheddar, finely grated

Fresh thyme – finely chopped (about a heaped teaspoon)

150ml buttermilk

Ground pepper (no added salt as the cheese has enough)

1 First light the oven – really hot 220°C – and place a baking sheet on the top shelf to preheat.

2 Sieve the flour and baking powder into a bowl and rub in the butter till fine.

3 Add pepper.

4 Stir in the grated cheese but keep back a little to put on top of the scones.

5 Add the buttermilk and mix well with a knife, then your hand to gather all the dry bits together.

6 Turn on to a lightly floured surface and knead very lightly.

7 Use the back of your hand or a rolling pin to flatten the dough to about ¾ inch or a good 2cm.

8 Flour the cutter and cut out the scones, re-rolling all the scrappy bits. Thank you to Ivy for her enthusiastic assistance.

9 Sprinkle a little of the remaining grated cheese on the top of each scone.

10 Take the hot tray out of the oven and sprinkle on a little flour, carefully place on the scones.

11 Get them straight into the oven and give them a good 10 minutes before you check them.

12 They will become nicely browned and the aroma in the kitchen will be amazing!

➲ Although dried thyme will be fine, using fresh really makes a noticeable difference.

➲ The beautiful 'faerdie maet' (picnic) box, made by Cecil Tait, is available at: **www.paparwark.com**

Pastel de Nata

During the first lockdown, in 2020, I signed up for a live online cookery class which was a fantastic experience. For two hours, together with 12 others from as far away as California, New York and Belgium, I was taught by João in his family bakery in Lisbon. Step by step, we went through each stage of making these delicious little custard tarts from scratch, with expert tuition as well as criticism. The elasticity and texture of the first stage of making the puff pastry dough was carefully scrutinised and commented upon, as well as the rolling out techniques, right to the final serving. (Do have a look at **www.eatwith.com**)

1 First, the pastry. I made mine by hand but you could use a stand mixer with a dough hook.

2 Put the flour and salt into the bowl and add the water slowly. Use a small palette knife and then your hand as the dough comes together. Knead steadily for another 10-12 minutes by which time the dough will be soft, smooth and elastic.

3 Dust the work surface with some flour and roll the dough out until it is just less than 1cm thick.

4 Place the butter, in a shallow block, in the centre and fold over the sides and top and bottom so they overlap in the centre.

5 Use the rolling pin to roll the dough into a rectangle about ½cm thick. Fold over one third from the top and again from the lower edge. Give the dough a quarter turn. Repeat this process. Then roll out once more.

6 Brush all over with cold water then roll up like a Swiss roll.

7 Wrap in baking parchment and put into the fridge while you make the custard.

8 Put the sugar and flour into a medium-sized bowl and put the milk, cinnamon stick and lemon peel into a pan to heat.

9 When the milk comes to the boil pour it slowly over the flour and sugar, mixing thoroughly with a whisk.

10 Return to the pan and bring slowly back to the boil, whisking constantly until the mixture thickens.

11 Remove from the heat, allow to cool to room temperature then beat in the egg yolks. Set aside.

12 Have ready a 12-hole shallow bun tin. Preheat the oven to 250°C – very hot.

13 Cut the rolled dough into 12 equal-sized pieces, with the coiled side uppermost.

14 Have a small bowl of water at hand, wet your thumb and press the dough into each of the tins, pushing it upwards so that the top edge of the pastry stands proud above the tin. (More room for more custard!)

15 Remove the lemon peel and cinnamon, give the custard a good whisk and pour into each tin.

16 Place into the hot oven near the top and, after 8-10 minutes, turn the tin to ensure even cooking.

17 Allow a further 6-7 minutes; the surface of the pastries will begin to rise and caramelise and the pastry will be puffed and golden. Shake the tray and if they wobble give them a further 2 minutes.

18 Remove the tray from the oven and allow the pastries to rest for 15 minutes before removing them from the tin. If you wish, sprinkle with a little ground cinnamon before eating.

Makes 12

Pastry

175g plain flour

1 level teaspoon salt

90g unsalted butter – at room temperature (this is important)

100ml water

Custard Filling

500ml full fat milk

50g plain flour

100g caster sugar

2 strips lemon peel

½ cinnamon stick

4 egg yolks

Ground cinnamon to decorate

Hazelnut Meringue and Ness Mess

There are so many eggs available all over Shetland in honesty boxes and, of course, sizes vary. It is therefore always safer to make meringue by weighing the ingredients. This is the recommended method of the fantastic baker Justin Gellatly, who started at the iconic St John in Smithfield, London. You will drool over his book, *Bread, Cake, Doughnut, Pudding.* For this method you need to use a stand mixer with a whisk attachment, as a phenomenal amount of whisking is involved.

Makes approximately 36 small meringues or 12 nests

100g egg whites

200g caster sugar

100g whole hazelnuts

Double cream and soft fruit to serve

1 First, deal with the roasted hazelnuts. Place them dry, in a heavy frying pan over a medium heat and shake them gently until they begin to colour. This may take 8-10 minutes. Allow them to cool and then place them in a clean tea towel and rub hard to remove most of the skins. Blitz them in a food processor to give a fine crumb.

2 Place the egg whites into the bowl of the mixer and whisk on high speed until the mixture is stiff (approximately 3-4 minutes), then add all of the sugar and continue whisking until really thick and glossy. This will take 8-10 minutes and will be noisy!

3 Carefully fold in the ground hazelnuts using a metal tablespoon until evenly incorporated.

4 Prepare two baking trays, each with a sheet of non-stick baking paper and preheat the oven to 120°C.

5 Use a piping bag with a wide nozzle, or a tablespoon, to make 'nests' on the baking tray – make some plain stars or neat spoonfuls, too.

6 Bake for about 1 hour, swapping trays over half way. The meringues should not brown.

7 Allow to cool and then use to make individual desserts with soft fruits and whipped cream, or a 'Ness Mess' with roughly broken meringue for a more informal dessert.

8 'Ness Mess' was created when one of my batches totally 'geed ta bruck' (broke apart)! I found greater success with hens' eggs rather than ducks' but your experience may be different. It *all* tastes delicious.

Gooseberry Frangipane

The gooseberry is another fruit that likes the Shetland climate. The bushes I have include the lovely variety Black Velvet – a deep purple dessert fruit which seems fairly resistant to sawfly, unlike the green variety which is regularly stripped of leaves. The frangipane mixture in this recipe can be made up to two days in advance and the dessert can be made in individual ramekins, as shown, or in one large ovenproof dish. This frangipane is so useful and is best with a strong flavoured tart fruit, so try with apple and blackberry, rhubarb, plum, damson or blackcurrant.

Makes 6

500g gooseberries – lightly cooked with 100g caster sugar (no water)

125g unsalted butter – at room temperature

125g caster sugar

125g ground almonds

6 drops almond essence

2 eggs, lightly beaten

15g flaked almonds – to decorate

1 Preheat oven to 180°C.

2 Put the cooked gooseberries into the ramekins.

3 Beat the sugar and butter till soft, then stir in eggs, almonds and essence.

4 Spoon over the gooseberries and sprinkle a few flaked almonds on top.

5 Bake for about 25 minutes, until lightly browned.

6 Allow to cool – best eaten just warm.

7 Yogurt or Shetland cream will make this easy dessert even more delicious.

➡ This is also a good dessert if you need a gluten-free option.

Baked Cheesecake with Hazelnut, Caramel and Apple

This cheesecake is rich and delicious with a great combination of flavours. Using toasted hazelnuts and oats in the base makes it gluten-free. It is also deliberately thin and not too sweet. The mixture of ricotta and cream cheese provides a good balance of creaminess and lightness. The celebrated Ukrainian author and cook Olia Hercules in her stunning book *Summer Kitchens* has a similar but lighter 'Curd Cake with Caramelised Apples' which is really delicious.

10 servings

Base

50g unsalted butter

100g fine oatmeal (or oat flour)

50g finely ground
toasted hazelnuts

15g demerara sugar

Filling

400g full fat cream cheese

350g ricotta

150g double cream

100g caster sugar

1 rounded teaspoon cornflour
(or gluten-free flour)

2 lemons – finely grated zest

4 eggs

Caramel

6 medium-sized tart eating apples

50g caster sugar

150g water

100g light soft brown sugar

50g unsalted butter

100ml double cream

Hazelnut Praline

50g toasted hazelnuts

100g granulated sugar

1 tablespoon water

1　Preheat the oven to 180°C. Grease a 23cm loose-bottomed cake tin.

2　Start with the base:

3　Melt 50g butter then add the oatmeal and ground hazelnuts; mix well.

4　Press into the base of the tin to form a thin layer.

5　Bake for 15 minutes, remove, then reduce the oven temperature to 120°C.

6　In a large bowl, mix all the filling ingredients together using a whisk. Alternatively, use a stand mixer

7　Pour over the base and bake for about 50-60 minutes.

8　Next, make a poaching syrup with 50g caster sugar and 150ml water and bring to the boil.

9　Peel, core and slice the apples and poach over a low heat for 2-3 minutes, until just barely cooked. Lift out the slices on to a plate.

10　Now make the caramel: put the soft brown sugar, butter and cream into a small pan and bring to the boil. Cook for 2-3 minutes, until thick, then allow to cool.

11　Finally, the praline: (have a sheet of baking paper ready); dissolve the granulated sugar in the water over a very low heat, then raise the temperature and cook until the colour begins to darken and the sugar caramelises. Add the hazelnuts and shake well until they are coated, then tip the whole lot onto the paper and allow to cool.

12　To assemble, lift the cheesecake on to a serving plate then spread a layer of the soft caramel over the top. Next, arrange the apple slices beautifully. Finally, use the hazelnut praline to decorate. I went for the rugged shard effect!

➔ The base can be made in advance.

Whole Orange and Almond Cake

You have to try this popular cake, where you make an orange purée by first boiling the oranges whole: skin, pith and juice. Also, with no flour and only four main ingredients it is easy to make and suitable for folk on a gluten-free diet. I used gluten-free baking powder, which is fairly easy to find in specialist shops or online; it is not essential but it does add a bit of lightness to the cake. You can, of course, use regular baking powder. The colour is really tremendous – not just because of the oranges but also from the Shetland free-range eggs I use from Scatness and Bigton which have such fantastic deep yellow yolks.

Serves 10-12

2 large oranges

6 eggs – lightly beaten

250g ground almonds

250g caster sugar

1 rounded teaspoon baking powder

This cake is best made in a sandwich tin (but you could use a loaf tin) and is lovely served on its own or with a spoonful of whipped cream or crème fraîche. Brushing the top with a little warmed marmalade or honey will give a beautiful shine. It is ideal as a dessert or can be dressed up as a birthday cake, garnished with thinly sliced orange segments.

1 First, prepare the oranges. Place them in a pan and cover them with cold water. Bring to the boil then turn down to a gentle simmer for 1 hour in total. Lift out and allow to cool slightly.

2 Next, line a 9" (23cm) round cake tin with baking parchment. Light the oven to 170°C.

3 Cut the whole oranges roughly (remove the pips) and pureé using either a stick blender or a food processor.

4 Put this pureé into a large mixing bowl, add the sugar, the ground almonds with the baking powder and finally beat in the eggs – a balloon whisk works best, I find.

5 Transfer the mixture to the prepared tin and bake in the centre of the oven for approximately 50-60 minutes. Check the cake after 30 minutes as you may need to lay a sheet of baking paper on top to prevent it over-browning.

6 Allow to cool slightly before transferring to a serving plate.

7 Brush the top with a little warmed honey for a lovely shine.

➲ This is a most reliable cake and one that I return to again and again.

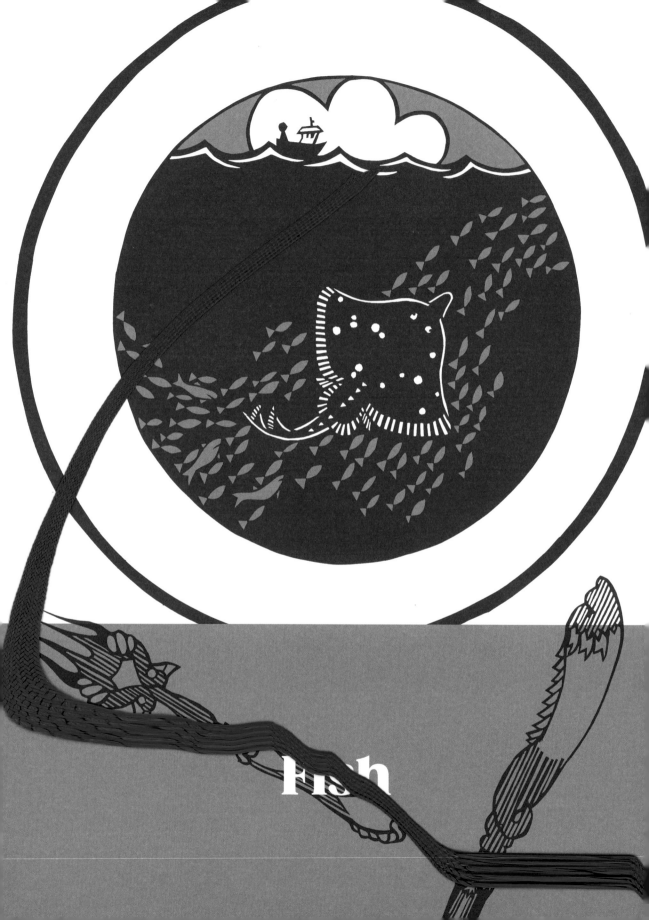

Fish

Shetland has a heritage and legacy of fishing which goes back 6,000 years – just look at the map as you travel around Shetland and it is clear why the sea has such influence. From modern piers and marinas full of peerie boats, to ancient evidence of boat 'noosts' on remote beaches, to the brand new fish markets in Lerwick and Scalloway which were opened in 2021 by the Prince of Wales, fishing plays a key part in the lives and livelihoods of so many folk in Shetland. It is also a source of great enjoyment: going 'aff' in a peerie boat on a fine summer's evening is one of life's great pleasures. One in five of the working population is directly employed in this thriving industry in three broad categories: the demersal, pelagic and inshore fleets, whose total value to the Shetland economy is over £350million a year. With the average age of a fisherman being 38, there is reason to be optimistic for the future of the industry.

At the Lerwick Fish Market, the Shetland Seafood Auction (**shetlandauction.com**) sells the fish caught by the local demersal or whitefish fleet. Over 20 modern boats (between 20-27 metres long) land on average 23 species on every working day. The electronic computerised 'Dutch auction' creates good prices for the fishermen and maintains the reputation for landing premium quality fish. Local and remote buyers from all over Europe and beyond, log in to buy on a regular basis. If you are a fish buyer you could register and buy too.

The pelagic fleet of eight vessels catch mackerel, herring and blue whiting. These boats are the largest in the fleet, mostly over 70 metres long, they operate very efficiently and are equipped to a very high standard. Their catches are in great demand and are usually frozen whole immediately after landing and then exported to Japan (mackerel in particular), Asia and Eastern Europe.

The inshore shellfish fleet of over 100 small boats measuring less than 10 metres catch scallops, lobsters, crabs and buckies. Many inshore fishermen are part-time with fishing providing a supplementary income. Most of the landings are exported to the continent with crabs and lobsters transported alive in specially designed tanks.

The Shetland Fishermen's Association plays a key role in making sure that the voice of Shetland fishermen is heard (**www.shetlandfishermen.com**). This is more important now than ever with the challenges of Brexit and quota making for unsettling times.

We are really fortunate to have in Scalloway, UHI Shetland (formerly the North Atlantic Fisheries College) which is a branch of the University of the Highlands and Islands (UHI). Their marine biologists sample and analyse essential data to support the fishing industry. In addition, courses are offered in many fishing-related subjects, including aquaculture, navigation and marine engineering. There is an excellent restaurant attached, Da Haaf, with a contemporary menu that champions local produce.

One fifth of the farmed salmon harvested in Scotland comes from the 44 marine sites in the tidal waters around Shetland, which employ over 400 people. Other businesses within Shetland provide engineering, manufacturing and support services, making the salmon industry very significant to the Shetland economy. Salmon is an affordable, highly nutritious and versatile fish which can be prepared and cooked with a variety of vegetables and seasonings to create really fast food.

Mussels are another great success story for Shetland. The Scottish Shellfish Marketing Group (SSMG) co-ordinates harvesting from nearly 20 sites around Shetland. Mussels grow slowly on ropes suspended from buoys in the pristine waters around the isles.

The two fish retailers Blydoit and Island Fish sell an excellent and changing selection of fresh and smoked fish according to what is on the market and will willingly seek out special requests too. Many Shetlanders, however, are rather cautious about choosing fish and 90% of all the white fish they regularly sell is haddock.

As an attempt to broaden the range of fish sold, the local seafood provenance scheme was created – do have a look at **www.tasteofshetland.com/explore/provenance**.

I hope you will be tempted to expand your recipe repertoire and seek out those species you might otherwise pass by: catfish, tusk, ling, witch, plaice, megrim – all available, fresh and delicious.

Hot Smoked Salmon with Citrus Marinade

Salmon is available throughout the year and farmed in the cold tidal waters of the voes around Shetland. The citrus marinade cuts through the richness perfectly and the hot smoking brings out the succulence and sharp flavours. Hot smoking is easy and quick – the Anuka smoker I use is available worldwide. Oatcakes are simple to make at home and provide a perfectly plain wholesome accompaniment. They keep well in an airtight tin.

Serves 10-12

Marinade for hot smoking

4 portions fresh salmon

4 tablespoons oil

Grated rind and juice of 1 orange

Grated rind and juice of 1 lemon

2 tablespoons finely chopped herbs: dill / parsley / tarragon

2 cloves garlic crushed and finely chopped

1 level teaspoon salt

3cm piece fresh ginger – coarsely grated

1 teaspoon grain mustard

1 teaspoon soft brown sugar

Oatcakes

75g medium oatmeal

75g fine oatmeal

½ teaspoon salt

25g butter melted with 2 tablespoons boiling water

1   Mix all the marinade ingredients in a shallow dish and coat the salmon – turning from time to time. Marinade overnight or for at least 6-8 hours.

2   Follow instructions on the smoker – depending on the thickness of the salmon smoking will take 20-40 minutes.

3   Best served warm or at room temperature with home-made oatcakes.

Oatcakes

1   Preheat oven to 150°C.

2   Mix everything to form a stiff dough. Use your hand to bring everything together.

3   Roll out thinly – about ½ cm thick – and form into a neat circle.

4   Cut into triangles and bake slowly for about 40 minutes – without browning – turning over halfway through cooking.

5   Cool on a wire rack and store in an airtight tin.

➲ Salmon is the ultimate versatile fast-food. It is really so quick to cook and as an oily fish is rich in Omega 3 and 6 fatty acids as well as vitamin B12 and potassium.

Pan-Fried Catfish with Turmeric and Smoked Paprika

This recipe is really simple, it looks attractive and tastes lovely, with a subtle smokiness from the smoked paprika. Turmeric is a member of the ginger family and it is the root that is eaten in a similar way to ginger. It has anti-inflammatory properties and provides a mild warmth. Catfish (sometimes called wolf fish) is an enormous and ugly species: it has dark skin and fearsome forehead. A number of years ago, in the iconic boat shed of the Shetland Museum & Archives, and accompanied by that legendary cook and writer Charlie Simpson, who was making stap*, I prepared this dish and others to an appreciative audience at Shetland Boat Week.

Serves 4

600g catfish fillets

2 rounded teaspoons
ground turmeric

2 rounded teaspoons
smoked paprika

2 rounded tablespoons beremeal
(white or rye flour would be fine)

1 level teaspoon salt

Plenty of freshly ground
black pepper

4 tablespoons rapeseed oil

In his book, *North Atlantic Seafood*, the late Alan Davidson refers to catfish as having 'great pavements of teeth ... in front, pointed like a tiger and behind, adapted for crushing.'

Its diet includes spiny sea urchins and crabs which contribute to its lovely flavour; hence its Icelandic name 'steinbitur', meaning stone biter. It is caught throughout the year around Shetland, usually sold as long, slender fillets and is generally very affordably priced.

1 Combine the turmeric, smoked paprika, beremeal and seasonings on to a flat plate or tray.

2 Cut the catfish into even-sized chunks and roll in the seasonings, pressing firmly.

3 Heat the oil in a large, shallow pan and fry in batches for about 5 minutes on each side.

4 Keep warm in a low oven until the pieces are all cooked.

5 Here, I have served these as a light lunch with couscous and spinach – they are equally delicious in a wrap with salad or as part of a mixed fish buffet.

★ Stap is a traditional mixture of two parts fish and one part livers – usually olick (ling) or piltock (saithe). Together with krappin – a mixture of fish livers and oatmeal – the recipes can be found in *Shetland Food and Cooking*.

Bacalao

This salt cod stew is my version of a really delicious traditional Portuguese classic dish. We are fortunate to have Thule Ventus' top quality salt cod produced to an incredibly high standard here in Shetland, and the local fishmongers also sell their traditional version from time to time. This recipe celebrates this delicious fish and the accompanying vegetables all complement the flavours and textures. It is also a one-pot meal and is even better if made a day ahead. It is a perfect dish for a crowd too: at John Goodlad's book launch of *The Cod Hunters* in the Shetland Museum and Archives, this was well received by the 80 guests.

Serves 4-6

200g dried salt cod

2 medium onions – sliced thinly

2 cloves garlic – crushed and finely chopped

3 tablespoons olive oil

1 red pepper – halved and deseeded

1 green pepper – halved and deseeded

500g potatoes – peeled, quartered and cooked until just done

1 tin chopped tomatoes

250g passata (sieved tomatoes)

Parsley (a large bunch) – coarsely chopped

15 black olives – pitted and halved (optional)

1 hard-boiled egg (optional)

1. Firstly, rinse the rock-hard salt cod to remove loose salt, then cover with cold water and soak for 24 hours. Change the water once.

2. Preheat the oven to 200°C.

3. Poach the soaked salt cod in fresh cold water – gently simmering for approx 10 minutes. Set aside on a dish and retain the water.

4. Toss the halved peppers in a tablespoon of olive oil, add salt and pepper and roast for approximately 10 minutes.

5. Soften the onions and garlic in a shallow pan with 2 tablespoons olive oil, over a low heat, for at least 15 minutes.

6. Add the tinned tomatoes and the passata and bring slowly to the boil. Simmer for 10 minutes and mix very well.

7. Taste, and add about 200ml of the soaking water, or plain water as required.

8. Add the salt cod, potatoes, peppers (sliced) and olives, mix gently and cook for 10 minutes – try to retain large, delicious flakes of salt cod. At this stage you can set the dish aside in a cool place overnight.

9. Serve piping hot with plenty of parsley and the chopped hard-boiled egg.

➔ Look out for John Goodlad's new book, *The Salt Roads: How Fish Made a Culture* .

Squid and Monkfish Linguine

Squid is definitely one of my top five favourite fish. Over the years I have eaten it on so many sunny summer holidays abroad, charred and delicious from a smoky barbecue. However, it can never be as fresh as here in Shetland, straight from the fish market. I love the texture and the versatility. There is so much more to enjoy about it than deep-fried rings which have often been frozen and can be tasteless. It is best to try and get whole squid and prepare it yourself. The tentacles are so attractive and the clear membrane is also astonishing – a great fish for a demonstration, especially with bairns where it really has the 'wow' factor.

Serves 4

300g small squid – cleaned and left whole; dried in kitchen paper

300g monkfish cut into chunks

1 large bulb fennel – shredded finely

1 large leek – split lengthways, washed and sliced fairly thinly

2 big cloves garlic – crushed and finely chopped

400g black linguine (plain is fine, as is spaghetti)

1 tablespoon capers

1 tablespoon double cream

Dill – a big handful, coarsely chopped (you could also use tarragon)

50g butter or sunflower/rapeseed oil

1 lemon – grated rind and juice

Salt and freshly ground black pepper

I use a large, shallow cast-iron pan for this dish, adding the cooked pasta at the end. Try, if you can, to get black linguine – coloured using squid ink and available at Scoop Wholefoods in Lerwick.

This dish makes a great centrepiece for an informal dinner. When cooking for the photo I used a ridged cast-iron pan to create attractive striping on the squid.

1   In a large pan, heat the butter or oil and cook the fennel over a fairly high heat until it begins to colour slightly.

2   Reduce the heat, add the leeks and garlic and cook slowly for about 10 minutes until soft. Lift out of the pan and set aside on a plate while you cook the fish.

3   Put a large pan of water on to boil for the pasta, adding a teaspoon of salt.

4   Cook the fish over a moderate to high heat, turning after 4-5 minutes.

5   Add the pasta to the pan of boiling water and cook until 'al dente' (10 minutes).

6   Return the fish to the frying pan and add the capers and lemon rind and juice.

7   Mix well and add salt and pepper to taste.

8   Drain the pasta (keep back some of the cooking liquid) and add to the pan. Add the tablespoon of cream and a little of the cooking water to create a delicious moist sauce.

9   Serve straight away with plenty of chopped dill.

Skate with Couscous, Roasted Carrot and Coriander

The wing of the skate (or ray) produces delicious sweet, long fibres of soft flesh. By lightly cooking the skate first and then removing all the fish from the flexible cartilage, there is absolutely no 'kerry-on' (fuss) with bones that sometimes puts people off eating fish. Carrots and coriander, both the seeds as well as the leaves, are complementary flavours and make a bright and colourful combination. Some of the carrots are made into a purée which makes this a lovely moist and tasty dish.

Serves 4

750g skate wing(s)

750g carrots

1 tablespoon double cream

2 tablespoons rapeseed oil

1 tablespoon coriander seeds – crushed in a pestle and mortar or roughly chopped

Small bunch coriander leaves – chopped roughly except for a few stalks for garnish

200g couscous

200ml vegetable stock (optional)

1 tablespoon olive oil or 15g butter

Salt and freshly ground pepper

1 Preheat the oven to Gas 200°C.

2 Cut 500g of the carrots into even-shaped pieces and place in a bowl with salt and freshly ground pepper, 1 tablespoon oil and the crushed coriander seeds. Mix well until lightly coated and transfer to a baking sheet.

3 Place on the top shelf of the oven and roast for approximately 15-20 minutes, until they are beginning to colour and are 'singing'. Remove from the oven.

4 Reduce the heat to 160°C.

5 Cut the remaining 250g carrots into chunks and boil in lightly-salted water until tender. Use a stick blender to make a purée. Add the cream and stir in a handful of chopped coriander leaves. Set aside.

6 Place the skate on to a lightly-oiled baking sheet and brush a little oil over the top. Season with salt and ground pepper. Bake for approx. 15-20 minutes at 160°C (turning once halfway through the cooking time) until the flesh is white and opaque.

7 Remove from the oven and allow to stand in a warm place, covered with a sheet of greaseproof paper or foil, for 10 minutes.

8 Using two forks, remove the flesh – try to keep in in large flakes.

9 Prepare the couscous by adding 200ml boiling water or stock to 200g couscous in a bowl with the olive oil or butter, mix well with a fork and allow to stand, covered with a plate, for 5-10 minutes.

10 Serve on warm plates, reheating the carrot purée until it is piping hot and placing the chunks of the lovely skate on top and the roasted carrots on the side.

11 Garnish with more coarsely chopped coriander.

➔ This recipe is one of the four recipe cards available from the Shetland Fishermen's Association to promote and encourage the cooking of lesser-used species.

Roasted Monkfish Tail with Stuffing

Here is a great recipe with robust flavours for this splendid fish which is caught in abundance around Shetland. Monkfish is a high-value fish and is landed throughout the year. It is prized for the firmness of its flesh and its ability to absorb strong flavours. The addition of anchovy and the moist stuffing makes this a real centrepiece dish for a special occasion. Thank you to Ivy and Magnus for helping with this terrific recipe.

Serves 4

1 monkfish tail – approx 750g

2 tablespoons oil

2 medium-sized onions – finely chopped

1 big clove garlic – crushed and finely chopped

2 slices bread (approximately 50g) – slightly stale and made into breadcrumbs (Waas Bakery taatie bread would be ideal)

1 handful fresh parsley – roughly chopped

Grated rind and juice of 1 lemon

1 tablespoon capers – chopped roughly

4 anchovy fillets

Freshly ground pepper

Salt to taste (remember the anchovies are salty)

25g butter

8 cherry tomatoes – halved

1 Prepare the fish: rub all over with a dribble of oil and season with salt and pepper.

2 Light the oven to 200°C.

3 Make the stuffing: soften the onion and garlic in the oil over low heat; this will take a good 15 minutes.

4 Add the breadcrumbs, lemon rind, capers and pepper. Mix well and set aside. Add lemon juice.

5 Put the monk tail on to a baking sheet and cut 4 deep slashes, but don't go right through.

6 Push an anchovy fillet deep inside each one and then add the stuffing. This job is best done with clean hands.

7 Put small pieces of butter down the length of the fish and top with the tomatoes.

8 Roast the fish on the top shelf for a good 15 minutes. Reduce the heat to 150°C for a further 5 minutes then remove from the oven and cover with a sheet of greaseproof paper. Leave for at least 15 minutes, during which time the heat will continue to cook the fish slowly.

9 Serve with boiled or steamed taaties and a seasonal green vegetable.

➲ Monkfish vary in size and thickness so these timings may need to be adjusted. However, a blast at high heat followed by a period of resting should produce a succulent and flavoursome dish.

Risotto with Smoked Haddock

Fresh haddock is Shetland's most popular and highest selling fish. The two Lerwick fish retailers (who also supply the network of independent local shops throughout Shetland) sell a very wide range of species but haddock accounts for over 90% of their sales. It is also the most popular ingredient of the best 'fish supper' readily available at the four fish and chip shops throughout Shetland. Smoked haddock is very popular in Shetland – smoking prolongs the shelf life and extends the use of the fish and opens up a whole spectrum of different dishes. Smoked haddock is a necessary ingredient in a good fish pie and in the delicious soup Cullen skink.* There is also this delicious classic risotto.

Serves 4

2 onions – finely chopped

50g Shetland butter

2½ litres chicken or vegetable stock

400g risotto rice – Carnaroli if possible

100g unsalted butter – cut into cubes

50g parmesan – finely grated

1 glass white wine (optional)

1   In a heavy-based pan, soften the chopped onion in 50g butter. Cook slowly until transparent – avoiding browning.

2   Have the stock ready and simmering in a separate pan.

3   Use some of it to gently poach the smoked haddock in a separate pan, and when just done, lift the fish out and set aside. (Use this flavoured poaching water in the risotto.)

4   Add the rice and stir so that the grains are well coated with butter.

5   Increase the heat and add the wine, which will soon evaporate.

6   Add the stock using a ladle, a ladleful at a time, stirring well with each addition.

7   The consistency should remain sloppy as the rice grains gradually soften and the starch is released. Taste and test regularly after about 15 minutes.

8   When almost done, and the rice still has a little bite, remove from the heat and gradually beat in the butter and then the grated parmesan.

9   Allow to rest for 2-3 minutes while you roughly flake the cooked smoked haddock.

10   Give a final stir and serve on warmed plates garnished with chopped parsley, tarragon or chives.

★ A legendary version of Cullen skink is made by (the Shetland) James Martin and served every Friday at The Peerie Shop Café on the Lerwick esplanade.

Crab Tart

In my view, the best way to eat crab is freshly caught and just cooked – both brown and white meat – with some salad leaves from the garden, newly-made bread and butter, a glass of cold white wine, sleeves rolled up and sitting in the lee of the house on a boanny simmer's (fine summer's) evening. That's not always possible, so crab pasta is another option, as is this tasty but rich and delicious tart.

Serves 6-8

200g plain flour

Large pinch salt

160g unsalted butter

1 egg yolk

2-3 teaspoons water

200g crab meat – brown and white together

3 eggs – lightly beaten

200ml full fat milk

100ml double cream

1   First, make the pastry: rub the butter into the flour and salt, add egg yolk and water to make a stiff paste.

2   Knead very lightly, roll out and line a 9" tin.

3   Allow to chill in the fridge, until the next day if necessary.

4   Preheat the oven to 190°C.

5   Brush a little beaten egg over the empty pastry case and bake for 10 minutes to seal and partly cook the pastry.

6   Thoroughly mix the eggs, milk, cream and crab meat together with a good grind of black pepper.

7   Add to the pastry case and bake near the top of the oven for 25 minutes, then check and reduce the heat for a further 10 minutes.

8   Allow to cool before serving.

9   A light salad or steamed vegetable is all that is required as an accompaniment.

⊙ The shellfish fisheries is managed by the Shetland Shellfish Management Organisation (www.ssmo.co.uk). They regulate catches and issue licences and sometimes implement periods of closure. Since 2012, Marine Stewardship Council (MSC) Accreditation, a sustainability standard, has been held for the Velvet Crab, Brown Crab and King Scallops fisheries. Shetland continues to have the only MSC certification for Brown Crab and dredged King Scallops of their kind in the world.

Hot Smoked Salmon Tarts

My baking tin of choice for these tarts is a four-hole Yorkshire pudding tin. The result is a perfect one-person sized tart with a good proportion of pastry to filling that is far quicker to cook than a larger quiche. The shape of the tins makes the pastry-lining stage not too fiddly and I find the results excellent for all kinds of sweet and savoury recipes. The spinach is really good in this recipe but leek would also be suitable. Whilst fresh spinach is best, I have had very good results with frozen leaf spinach, which is also very convenient. Be sure to heat it thoroughly first and drain off all the water.

Makes 8

Pastry

200g plain flour

100g unsalted butter

7-8 teaspoons cold water

Large pinch salt

Filling

200g hot smoked salmon

100g cooked spinach

2 eggs

200ml full-fat milk

Ground pepper

1   Firstly, make the pastry by hand or in a mixer: rub the butter into the floured salt, add the water, mix to a stiff paste, knead lightly, roll out thinly and cut out circles to fit the tins (you will probably have to use a small bowl for this as most cutters are not big enough).

2   Press carefully into the tins and then put them into the fridge to chill while you get on with the filling.

3   Preheat the oven to 180°C.

4   Lightly mix together the egg and milk and add a pinch of salt and ground black pepper.

5   Thoroughly squeeze out any water from the spinach – use kitchen paper to absorb any excess.

6   Place the spinach and flaked salmon into each tin, pour in the egg and milk mixture and bake near the top of the oven for approximately 15-20 minutes. Check after 15 minutes and rotate the tins if necessary.

7   Serve warm.

★ See the Hot Smoked Salmon recipe on page 66 if you would like to make your own.

Gravad Mackerel with Dill Cream Sauce

This is the mackerel version of the well-loved gravadlax (cured salmon with dill) and it is truly delicious. With such a quantity of fresh mackerel available from peerie (small) boats in the summer, this is a really good way to preserve a few of them. I am indebted to Jan Riise and Kenny Pottinger for their their advice with this recipe. The dill crème fraiche sauce to accompany this is creamy and rich but the traditional dill mustard sauce is fine to use too. Warning: this is a three-day process. First, go to the beach and 'gadder' some large stanes! I'm joking! Any heavy weight will be fine.

Serves 4 as a starter

6 fresh mackerel fillets – filleted and skinned

25g demerara sugar

25g coarse salt (table salt will be fine)

Small handful fresh dill

Coarsely ground black pepper

Sauce

1 tub crème fraiche – 225g

Small bunch dill – finely chopped

1 rounded teaspoon demerara sugar

Day 1

Lay the fillets in pairs in a shallow dish with the curing mixture between them. Add a suitable-sized smaller dish on top and weigh it down with fine Shetland beach stones. Leave in a cool place and check each day, turning them over and making sure that the curing mixture – which will now be very liquid – is reaching all the fish.

Day 3 (or 4)

Mix the sauce ingredients thoroughly and transfer to a small dish.

Scrape the peppercorns and dill off the fillets and pat them dry with kitchen paper.

Slice thinly at an angle and serve with the sauce on oatcakes, rybread or a dark beremeal bannock.

❶ This makes a great starter or a snack and it keeps really well in the fridge.

Baked Hake Niçoise with Root Vegetable Mash

Hake is a popular fish with a beautifully white, soft flesh when cooked. Large quantities are landed throughout the year in Shetland. The fish has a dark, tough skin which is best removed before cooking. The flavour is delicate and it is usually moderately priced. In many fish shops and supermarkets on mainland UK much of the hake sold is caught in South Africa. Why?

Serves 4 (or 6 as a starter)

500g taaties

250g neep, parsnip or celeriac

2-3 tablespoons milk

25g Shetland butter

6 small cherry tomatoes – cut into slices (optional)

600g hake fillet – cut into chunks

1 clove garlic – crushed and finely chopped

50g Shetland butter

10 anchovy fillets

6 stoned olives

Dill or tarragon to garnish

1   First, make the root vegetable mash: boil the vegetables till soft, then mash until semi-smooth with the milk and butter. Taste and add salt and freshly ground pepper as necessary.

2   Preheat the oven to 220°C.

3   In a frying pan, melt the butter and cook the garlic until soft but not browned. Add the hake and cook on both sides for 2-3 minutes. (It will not be fully cooked through.) Add the sliced cherry tomatoes and simmer very gently for 2-3 minutes.

4   Place mounds of mash on to a sheet of greaseproof paper on a baking tray and make a dip in the centre. Bake on the top shelf until beginning to turn brown and crispy (approx 15-20 minutes).

5   Carefully remove from the oven and reduce the heat to 150°C.

6   Put a spoonful of the garlicky tomatoes into each dip, then pieces of the hake on top.

7   Add anchovies and olives in a criss cross pattern.

8   Bake for approximately 15-20 minutes, until the fish is just cooked.

9   Garnish with dill or tarragon and serve hot.

Stuffed Squid with Raisins and Pine Nuts

This is a dish inspired by the cooking of Spain and Portugal whose fish recipes include some ingredients to which a Shetlander might not immediately turn to. I really admire the writing of Elizabeth Luard and this is one of her ideas, which I have adapted for Shetland squid. Do not be put off by the use of a little cinnamon together with the raisins and pine nuts – the flavours really do work together, even far from the Mediterranean.

Serves 4-6 as a main course

900g whole fresh squid – small-medium sized if possible

1 large onion – finely chopped

1 clove garlic – crushed and finely chopped

2 tablespoons olive oil

50g pine nuts

50g raisins

Level teaspoon ground cinnamon

75g fresh white breadcrumbs

Rind and juice of a lemon

Pinch saffron threads – soaked in a tablespoon warm water

50ml olive oil (for cooking)

150ml white wine

1 First, prepare the squid: separate the body from the head and entrails, wash thoroughly and cut off the tentacles. Chop half of them into small pieces – these will be used in the stuffing and to garnish. Season with salt and ground black pepper and a squeeze of lemon juice, and set aside.

2 Make the stuffing by cooking the onion and garlic in 2 tablespoons oil till soft. Add the chopped tentacles, lemon rind and juice, cinnamon, pine nuts and raisins and mix well. Season with a little salt and pepper. Stir in the breadcrumbs.

3 Carefully spoon the stuffing into the squid bodies – do not over-stuff. Close with a cocktail stick or thin skewer.

4 In a heavy shallow pan, heat the oil, white wine and saffron, then lay in the stuffed squid and bring to the boil. Immediately, turn down the heat and simmer gently for about 20 minutes, turning the squid so that they cook evenly.

5 Serve with bread or bannocks with some of the brö (cooking broth) reduced slightly if necessary.

6 A lovely green salad would be good here too.

Mussels with Coconut, Spring Onion and Ginger

Shetland produces about 80% of all the mussels sold in the UK and a considerable quantity of the UK's export market too. It's not hard to see why: fast-flowing, clean, cold water and people who are experienced, passionate and proud to produce this high quality product. Everyone has their favourite way of cooking and serving mussels and, in many ways, doing absolutely nothing is simplest and best, but here is an idea for you to try that has proved very popular with our family.

Serves 2

500g bag live mussels

15g butter

25g piece fresh ginger – thinly sliced into matchsticks

1 clove garlic – crushed and finely chopped

4 spring onions – thinly sliced

½ can coconut milk – approx 200ml

Chopped parsley

1   First, prepare the mussels: rinse thoroughly in cold water and pull off the loose 'beards'. Discard any that do not close.

2   In a very large pan, melt the butter and slowly cook the garlic, spring onion and ginger until soft, but not browned.

3   Add the coconut milk and bring to the boil. Cook for 2-3 minutes.

4   Tip in the mussels and put the lid on firmly. Cook for 2-4 minutes, giving a good shake halfway through.

5   Check that the mussels are open and cook for a further minute or two if necessary.

6   Serve immediately with plenty of chopped parsley sprinkled over.

➔ I have been delighted to work with Shetland Select mussels over the last few years. This small family business has harvested exclusively from Basta Voe in Yell and also shortly from Vementry, to the west of Shetland. These premium mussels are hand selected and have a closed season in order to protect stocks. They supply the high-end restaurant trade in both the UK and the Middle East.

Herring Under a Fur Coat

This is a Russian recipe with a fabulous combination of ingredients that all beautifully complement cured herring. For many years I have been interested in the food of Russia and, in 1975, in my fourth year at the Edinburgh College of Domestic Science, our final project was a study of, and presentation featuring classic Russian dishes. This is basically a cold layered salad incorporating beetroot, potatoes, carrots, eggs, herring, onion, dill and mayonnaise. The supposed history of the name originated with a Moscow bar owner who, around 1919, needed something to keep his patrons from becoming too intoxicated; one of his chefs came up with the dish and named it SHUBA which happens to mean "fur coat". The people loved it, and the name morphed into herring under a fur coat.

Serves 4

4 cured herring fillets and 4 slices of onion from the jar; alternatively, use 2 finely chopped shallots

2 beetroots – cooked

4 medium-sized waxy potatoes – cooked and skinned

6 tablespoons mayonnaise – best quality or homemade

2 medium-sized carrots – cooked

2 hard-boiled eggs – shelled and the yolks and whites separated

Salt and freshly ground pepper

Plenty of dill – for garnish

1   Once all the ingredients are prepared, it is a straightforward assembly task.

2   Use a little of the mayonnaise to mix with each layer.

3   Finely dice the herring fillets and the onion from the jar (or shallots).

4   Chop the egg white and finely grate or sieve the egg yolk.

5   Using the coarsest side of the grater, grate the potato then, separately, the carrots and finally the beetroot.

6   Mix half the beetroot with 2 tablespoons mayonnaise. This will result in a fantastic pink-coloured mixture.

7   Mix the grated potato with 2 tablespoons mayonnaise.

8   Have the moulds ready and start layering: there is no strict order but I found that potato mixture makes a good solid base.

9   So, potato, herring and onion with some dill, carrot, beetroot with mayonnaise, beetroot, then, finally, the egg white round the edge and the yolk in the centre.

10 Garnish with plenty of finely chopped dill.

Cured Herring

Here are two different but delicious cured herring recipes. Recipe 1 is from my fellow director at Shetland Food and Drink, Bo Simmons, who is a talented, experienced and creative cook and author. The herring in this recipe will keep for up to a year. Recipe 2 is from Johnny Simpson, fisherman and keen cook, who kindly supplied fine herring for my recipe testing. In this recipe, the fish should be eaten within two weeks.

Recipe 1

1   For 20 skinned herring fillets (10 herring). Place the fillets in a shallow dish (china, glass or enamel is best) and pour over a mixture of 100ml water and 100ml distilled malt vinegar. Leave overnight.

2   Mix together 450g salt, 225g brown sugar, 2 tablespoons crushed peppercorns, 1 tablespoon crushed allspice and 2-3 bayleaves – roughly torn.

3   Drain the herring on kitchen paper, rinse the dish and then layer the herring fillets with this mixture. Weigh down with a plate or another dish (maybe those beach stones again) and leave for 24 - 48 hours.

4   Sweet pickle. Make a syrup by gently heating: 225g brown sugar, 150ml cider vinegar, 8 peppercorns and a teaspoon pickling spice. Stir until sugar is dissolved and then allow to cool.

5   Meanwhile, rinse the salt/sugar mixture off the fish, cut into bite sized pieces if preferred and soak in 100ml milk and 100ml water while syrup is cooling.

6   Wash and sterilise 2 medium sized jars.

7   Slice 2 medium sized red onions, 5 pickled gherkins and a small handful of dill or fennel leaves.

8   Dry the herring and layer in the jars with the cold syrup, onion and gherkin.

9   Leave for 48 hours before eating. Will keep up to 1 year.

Recipe 2

1   For 20 skinned herring fillets (10 herring). Place the fillets in a shallow dish and sprinkle over approximately 3-4 tablespoons salt. Leave overnight.

2   Mix together (in the proportions of 3:2:1) 600ml distilled malt vinegar, 400g brown sugar and 200ml water. Stir well to dissolve the sugar.

3   Slice 2 medium sized onions and 1 tablespoon peppercorns, slightly crushed.

4   Rinse the herring and cut into bite sized pieces if preferred.

5   Wash and sterilise 2 medium sized jars.

6   Layer the fish, onion and peppercorns and leave 3-5 days before using. Use within 2-3 weeks.

Fresh Salmon Koftes with Horseradish Sauce

Alongside the recipe for scallops, these would be ideal for a starter, a fish buffet or a 'small plates' occasion. They are like little 'burgers' and are another super idea for using fresh salmon – one of Shetland's key products and a major export commodity. They are ideal for using up offcuts or misshapen pieces of fish. In this recipe I am using gram flour so that these can be gluten-free. Beremeal or wholemeal flour would also be fine. Do use plenty of dill. For the horseradish sauce, if you are able to grow your own horseradish root then finely grate about 2 tablespoons, well chopped, into 4 tablespoons double cream, the flavours will be in another stratosphere!

Makes 6

250g fresh salmon – skinned and cut into chunks

25g gram flour

Small bunch (20g) fresh dill – finely chopped

Salt and freshly ground black pepper

25g butter or oil for frying

Horseradish sauce to serve

1 lemon to serve

1 Place the pieces of salmon into a food processor or similar and process briefly, or use a sharp knife, so that the fish is roughly chopped.

2 In a mixing bowl, put the salmon, dill, gram flour, salt and pepper. Mix well.

3 Sprinkle a little of the gram flour onto the work surface and shape the mixture into small koftes, as shown.

4 In a heavy-based pan, melt the butter and cook the koftes until they are lightly browned – 4-5 minutes on each side. Allow to stand for 5 minutes and serve warm or at room temperature.

These tasty morsels can also be eaten in a wrap with salad or, as shown, with a vegetable or salad and a good squeeze of lemon.

Pan-Fried Scallops with Tarragon, Cream and Capers

Like most shellfish, simple really is best. Here is an idea using some of my favourite combinations of ingredients. Be sure to buy scallops with their corals, for flavour, colour and sustainability. When cooking scallops, the heat should be pretty fierce to encourage caramelisation of the outside, so don't be afraid to have the pan screaming hot. The outside should be nicely browned and the centre will be soft and tender. In the photograph I have served the scallops with some red Camargue rice and broccoli as a light lunch idea.

Serves 2

6 scallops, including corals

50g butter

Small bunch fresh tarragon – coarsely chopped

2 teaspoons capers

4 tablespoons double cream

4 tablespoons cooked speciality rice – red or black looks dramatic

Broccoli, or similar, to accompany

1 Heat the butter in a heavy frying pan and add the scallops, well spread apart. Allow to cook 2 or 3 minutes until browned and then turn over with tongs and repeat.

2 Lift on to a warm serving plate and add the capers, cream and chopped tarragon and mix well. Add a splash of hot water to create a little bit of sauce and spoon carefully over the scallops.

3 Put the cooked rice into the pan now, to soak up all the juices. Taste and add a little more water or a squeeze of lemon juice if necessary.

4 Heat thoroughly and plate immediately, garnishing with the remaining tarragon, and serve with a vegetable or salad of your choice.

The beautiful platter is made in North Roe by talented ceramicist Sharon McGeady – her work is available through Shetland Arts or at Ninian in Lerwick.

Meat

Meat production in Shetland is buoyant, with good prices at the local marts. This is a live auction, open to the public, and it is so interesting to watch crofters and farmers sell their animals in person, interact with buyers and display their pride in the quality of the animals they have reared. This, in turn, has resulted in a considerable increase in the numbers of animals slaughtered and processed locally – a real boost for the economy. There is also a strong and lively young farmers' group who are proactive and forward looking – so the future looks to be in safe hands.

I have often written about my strong support for the abattoir – absolutely essential for Shetland in order to maintain the true local provenance that our home-reared meat enjoys. There are very few small abattoirs like ours in rural communities and without doubt the service provides huge benefits, most importantly for animal welfare but also for the support of those involved in meat production who often operate on a really small scale.

The abattoir also enables our native breed of small lambs to have the Protected Designation of Origin (PDO), recognising that it is pure bred, born, raised and slaughtered here.

This is the best lamb of all – sweet and succulent meat. The hardy animals often eat seaweed (nowhere in Shetland is more than three miles from the sea) but unlike those that are cross-bred, they actually thrive on the hills where all the natural wild herbs and heathery plants grow.

The lamb season is from September through to December. This is when animals are slaughtered and prepared for sale and for the freezer – for autumn and winter meals and beyond. The native lamb also matures beautifully, first to hog (usually over 12 months "with two or more permanent incisors in wear") and then to mutton – which could be up to four years old. At this stage the flavour is strong and the flesh tougher but, my goodness, what delicious slow-cooked meals can be had.

Of the three mainstays of the abattoir – kye (cows), sheep and pigs – there has been a particularly large increase in pork production, and of excellent quality too. Many more folk are keeping pigs on a small scale because they want meat that tastes good, is local, well looked after and also helps reduce kitchen food waste. There is no poultry produced locally – hence no recipes in this book.

Most of the beef reared in Shetland is from cross-bred animals which are more economical to produce as the carcass is larger. Many folk who can, buy a quarter or eighth of an animal for the freezer – crofters and farmers usually advertise locally when available. The pure native breed, however, produces beef which is exceptionally succulent and full of flavour. This is available in much smaller quantities and is very much worth seeking out for its excellent eating qualities.

There is a thriving meat retail sector in Shetland with big recent investment from the Scalloway Meat Company which has shops in Lerwick and Scalloway.

Young farmer Jakob Eunson's native organic meat is sold directly or from Scoop Wholefoods in Lerwick; and a new retail shop, Sound Butchers (adjacent to the Blydoit fish shop), is about to start marketing their unique Lamb Biltong. The long established family business, Anderson Butchers, continues to operate in Whiteness. Each of these businesses makes their own unique selections of pies, sausages and cold meats, and they all deliver supplies several times a week to the network of independent shops throughout Shetland. Many of the recipes here use the more economical cuts of meat and are best made a day ahead.

Slow Cooked Beef Cheeks with Fragrant Spices

These beef cheeks are sliced and cooked slowly with a selection of light fragrant spices (only a little heat from the ginger). Beef cheeks are easily available from the butcher – the meat is gelatinous and makes a wonderful gravy – but long, slow cooking is essential. They're ideal, too, for making in advance. A simple creamy mash of taaties and celeriac adds great flavours. All that is necessary as an accompaniment is some lightly cooked greens. Shetland kale is a traditional favourite and cavolo nero is equally good with dramatically dark green leaves and a lovely texture.

Serves 6

2 tablespoons rapeseed oil

2 beef cheeks (approx. 800g) cut into large pieces across the grain of the meat

2 medium onions – roughly chopped

2 cloves garlic – crushed and chopped

2 sticks celery – cut into 2cm pieces

2 bay leaves

1 piece fresh ginger (about 2cm) – thinly sliced

2 star anise

1 piece cinnamon stick (about 5cm)

½ teaspoon juniper berries (about 10) – crushed

Cloves – about 6

Level teaspoon salt

Freshly ground black pepper

1 x 400g tin chopped tomatoes + the tin rinsed out with cold water

2 medium-sized carrots cut into large chunks (add for the last hour of cooking)

200g neep (turnip) cut into large chunks (add for the last hour of cooking)

Small bunch fresh parsley – roughly chopped

1   Preheat the oven to 150°C.

2   Heat the oil in an ovenproof casserole pot and brown the pieces of meat all over. Set aside.

3   Cook the onion, garlic, celery until the onion is soft – about 10 minutes over a low heat.

4   Add all the spices and mix well. Then add the tinned tomatoes and water.

5   Return the meat to the pot and bring to the boil, adding more water if necessary – the meat should be just covered.

6   Season with salt and pepper.

7   Cover with a well-fitting lid and cook for approximately 3 hours, reducing the heat to 120°C after the first hour. Add the carrots and neeps for the last hour.

8   This casserole is perfect for making in advance. Serve with mash and greens.

Lechon Asado
Cuban Roast Pork with Orange and Rum

There is such a lot of really good pork being produced in Shetland at the moment; animal welfare standards are high and, as the animals are slaughtered at the Lerwick abattoir, food miles are low. Whilst apple and sage are the usual accompanying flavours for a traditional roast pork, these more lively ingredients lend a lovely tang to the cooked roast – and the aromas are fantastic. The acidity from the oranges also tenderises the meat. This is not a roast to rustle up quickly. Ideally, prepare the day before and marinade overnight, then the results will be particularly delicious.

Serves 4-6

1.5kg piece of shoulder
– skin removed but with
about 1cm fat remaining

1½ tablespoons cumin seeds
– lightly dry-roasted

½ tablespoon black peppercorns

6 cloves garlic

1 tablespoon dried oregano

1 teaspoon salt

Using a pestle and mortar or similar, grind all the above ingredients to a paste before adding the following:

Grated rind and juice of 2 oranges (Seville if possible) and a lemon

2 tablespoons dark rum

2 tablespoons oil

1   Mix all the marinade ingredients together.

2   Using a sharp knife pierce the meat deeply and rub in the spice mixture.

3   Ideally leave overnight.

4   Preheat the oven to 220°C and cook, uncovered, for 30 minutes, then cover with foil and reduce the heat to 160°C for about another 1½ hours.

5   Remove from the oven and allow to rest on a dish, covered, for at least 20 minutes.

6   Meanwhile, add 125ml stock or water (and a dash of rum if you like) to the roasting tin and bring to the boil. Strain this into a jug and serve with the meat.

Saasermaet Meatballs in Tomato Sauce

Saasermaet has evolved considerably since I was a small child. This traditional spiced sausagemeat is widely produced in Shetland and each butcher has their own secret recipe. A thick slice in a soft roll has sustained many a soul after the long celebrations of Up-Helly-Aa and several catering units around Shetland offer a saasermaet roll as a fast takeaway option. It can be made with beef or pork.

Serves 6

300g lean minced beef

300g pork saasermaet

2 cloves garlic – crushed and finely chopped

50g fresh parsley – roughly chopped

10g chives – finely snipped

1 rounded teaspoon dried oregano

1 level teaspoon salt

Plenty of freshly ground black pepper

1 tablespoon fine oatmeal

1 egg – lightly beaten

Mix everything together really well and shape into balls about the size of a walnut. Set aside in a cool place or in the fridge.

Tomato Sauce

2 medium-sized onions – finely chopped

2 cloves garlic – crushed and finely chopped

2 tablespoons sunflower or rapeseed oil

3 tablespoons parsley – roughly chopped

2 teaspoons dried oregano

1 tin chopped plum tomatoes + 1 tin water

500g passata (sieved tomatoes)

1 tablespoon balsamic vinegar

1 level teaspoon salt

Plenty of freshly ground pepper

I find that mixing it with leaner meat cuts the richness whilst preserving the unique taste which is provided by, amongst other things, mace, allspice and white pepper (See *Cookery for Northern Wives* for an authentic recipe.) This recipe is a huge favourite in our family, particularly with the grandchildren, who are easily persuaded to help make it, too. The meatballs are not fried, but cooked in a delicious rich tomato sauce. Do not hold back on the fresh herbs, they really contribute to the flavours and appearance.

1   Soften the onion and garlic slowly in the oil in a large, shallow, lidded ovenproof casserole for 10-15 minutes.

2   Add all the other ingredients and slowly bring to the boil. Reduce the heat and cook gently for 15 minutes. Stir really well.

3   One by one, drop the meatballs into the sauce and allow to come up to boiling point. Reduce the heat and simmer with the lid on for about 20 minutes.

4   Give the whole dish a very gentle stir – be careful not to break up the meatballs – then replace the lid and turn off the heat.

5   Allow the casserole to stand for 20 minutes undisturbed while you get on with the rest of the meal.

6   This dish can be made well in advance and can be frozen in smaller quantities – ideal for quick child dinners.

7   These meatballs go really well with mashed taaties, a mixture of taaties and other root vegetables, or with pasta, rice or couscous.

8   Before serving, garnish with plenty of freshly chopped chives.

➲ Jakob Eunson at Uradale Farm makes very good saasermaet from his organically-reared native Shetland kye. It is a bit leaner and very nicely spiced.

Picnic Lamb Pasties

Shetland lamb, neeps (swede), carrots and taaties (potatoes), seasoned and enclosed in shortcrust pastry. Not as fast as making sandwiches, but so very tasty to have on a really good long walk or as part of a beach picnic. Experience shows me that the vegetables should be parboiled but the lamb uncooked. Other suitable vegetables are parsnip and celeriac. It is, of course, easy to make these without meat, and to make vegan pastry substitute the butter for a vegan spread or oil.

Makes 6

Pastry

150g plain flour

75g unsalted butter

Freshly ground black pepper

5-6 teaspoons cold water

Beaten egg to glaze

Filling

1 medium-sized taatie
– peeled quartered and
parboiled for 5 minutes

1 piece neep (approx 100g) –
peeled and parboiled for 5 minutes

1 medium-sized carrot – peeled
and parboiled for 5 minutes

150g lamb (leg or shoulder)
– cut into small dice

1 level teaspoon ground
cumin (optional)

1 level tablespoon finely
chopped fresh herbs (rosemary
or thyme) – dried is also fine

Salt and freshly ground
black pepper

1 Firstly make the shortcrust pastry: rub the butter into the flour until the mixture resembles fine breadcrumbs, add the water, mix well, knead lightly.

2 Roll out thinly and cut 6 circles approx 15cm in diameter. Spread them out on a baking tray layered with baking paper and put into the fridge to rest while you get on with the filling.

3 Preheat the oven to 200°C.

4 In a bowl, mix together the part-cooked vegetables and cubed meat. Add salt and pepper, herbs and the cumin, if using. Mix well and divide between the 6 pastry circles.

5 Wet the edges with cold water and press firmly into the traditional pastie shape.

6 Brush with beaten egg and bake for a total of 45 minutes, turning the oven down to 150°C after 20 minutes.

7 Eat warm.

Lamb Flank with Balsamic Vinegar

I am indebted to my fellow Shetland Food and Drink director, Eric Graham, for this recipe as well as for his excellent lamb reared at Gremista Farm, Lerwick. Flank or breast of lamb is a lesser-used cut that requires long, slow cooking and has good strong flavours. This recipe certainly delivers that. The balsamic vinegar adds a lovely sweetness and the accompanying flageolet beans – with their lovely pale green colour – add to the rustic, attractive presentation. There is no fine dining here; rolled up sleeves and eating off the bones is definitely allowed.

Serves 4

1 lamb flank – approximately 1 kg

225ml balsamic vinegar
– basic quality

225ml water

3 cloves garlic – cut in half

500ml stock – lamb or chicken

2 tins cooked flageolet
beans – well rinsed

Salt and ground black pepper

1 Preheat the oven to 150°C.

2 Place the flank in a small roasting tin skin side up and add the water, stock, garlic and balsamic vinegar.

3 Cover with greaseproof paper or foil and cook for 3-4 hours in the centre of the oven.

4 Remove from the oven, sprinkle a teaspoon of sea salt over the skin and increase the temperature to 190°C for a further 30 minutes to brown the skin.

5 Lift the meat out of the roasting tin and set aside on a warmed ashet.

6 Add the 2 tins flageolets to the cooking juices, stir well and heat through thoroughly. Taste, and adjust seasoning.

7 Cut the flank into slices and serve on the beans.

8 This is delicious served with shappit (mashed) taaties and steamed Shetland kale.

➲ Instead of canned you could use dried beans which should be soaked overnight then simmered for approximately 2 hours.

Smoked Lamb

The tradition of making reestit mutton* originally involved the salted meat hanging in the 'reest' or rafters, usually above an open peat fire or peat-fired Rayburn or equivalent. The smoking aspect doesn't happen in the process used today for reestit mutton for general sale. Smoked lamb is, though, delicious. I always seek it out when visiting family in Iceland, where it is available in the piece or thinly sliced to have with some of their delicious flatcakes. One of my fellow directors at Shetland Food and Drink, Chris Percival, was the first winner of the 'Shetland Cooking Challenge' (subsequently renamed 'Muckle Bites'). Part of the main course from his memorable menu involved a trio of lamb, one of which was heather-smoked on the hob, creating the delightful waft of a Shetland hill from the demonstration kitchen at the final cook-off. It was totally delicious and no fire alarms were activated.

Serves 10-15 as a snack

1 piece rolled shoulder of lamb or a whole fillet of lamb, approx 500g

40g salt

500ml water

Peppercorns

Bay leaf

Many Shetlanders have a home smoker – sometimes homemade. I've got a small electric hot smoker, supplied locally, which I use for mackerel, herring and salmon. Here, I have tried to recreate, on a domestic scale, the salty, smoky taste of the reestit mutton I remember from my childhood.

1   Place the meat in a deep dish with the salted water.

2   Leave for three days, turning occasionally to ensure the meat is submerged.

3   If using the shoulder, cut into 2cm thick slices. For the fillet, cut into 3 or 4 lengths.

4   Prepare smoker and smoke for 25 minutes.

5   Turn the pieces of meat over and smoke for a further 20 minutes.

6   Allow to cool down in the smoker.

7   Slice very thinly, and treat like prosciutto. Delicious as an aperitif, as a snack or as part of a sharing platter, starter or smorgasbord.

★ You can see a short film explaining the process on the Taste of Shetland YouTube channel. Search for "Taste of Shetland Food Heritage Film - Reestit Mutton".

Bunny Chow

Bunny Chow, is a South African dish consisting of a hollowed out loaf of bread filled with curry, which can be meat or vegetable. It originated in the Durban Indian community and is still a popular and filling takeaway. I am indebted to Dr Kushik Lala, consultant in A&E medicine at the Gilbert Bain Hospital, Lerwick for his advice and guidance, and to Anusha Cele, senior children's nurse at the KwaDukuza hospital. Also to my son, Alexander, who first introduced me to Bunny Chow in a cafe in Stanger, KwaZulu-Natal and set up 'Bunny International' on WhatsApp in order that Anusha and I could discuss fine details!

Serves 2 with leftovers

1 small loaf white bread

1kg lamb pieces from the neck or shoulder, including bones

2 level teaspoons salt

2 tablespoons sunflower oil

2 pieces cinnamon stick (10cm)

1 teaspoon fennel seeds

6 cloves

1 bay leaf

6 green cardamoms

3 or 4 curry leaves (if available)

1 small green chilli – deseeded

1 level teaspoon turmeric

1 level teaspoon ground cumin

1 level teaspoon ground coriander

1 level teaspoon medium chilli powder

1 level tablespoon sugar

50g fresh ginger – grated or finely sliced

2 cloves garlic – crushed and finely chopped

2 medium-sized onions – finely chopped

1 lemon – grated rind and juice

Fresh tomatoes – 200g (I used small cherry tomatoes)

200ml passata (sieved tomatoes)

4 medium-sized potatoes

1 Preheat the oven to 150°C.

2 Heat the oil in a heavy casserole dish. Add all of the spices, ginger, garlic and onions and cook slowly to release the most amazing aromas.

3 Add the sugar, lemon rind and juice. Add the meat and salt and mix very well.

4 Add tomatoes and passata and bring to the boil. Reduce heat and cook slowly in the oven for about 2 hours. After 1 hour add the potatoes, cut into quarters. The curry should have quite a lot of delicious sauce.

5 To serve: cut the loaf in half and then hollow out the centre and slice into pieces. These, like sponges, will mop up the juices. Fill the centre with the curry and enjoy.

6 Traditionally, a side salad is included.

7 Wrapped in greaseproof, this will transport well and keep hot for a while.

➲ Which Shetland walk would you like to do with one of these in your faerdie-maet (picnic) box?

Pulled Pork Wraps

This is such a great recipe, perfect for a substantial picnic on a fine long walk or to feed hungry bairns on an evening at the beach. The pork is cooked slowly in a mildly sweet and spicy marinade, either in a slow-cooker or in a very slow oven for 4-5 hours. You can, of course, buy the wraps, but do try making your own – it's really easy. The inspiration for these wraps comes from Sheila Keith, one of my fellow directors at Shetland Food and Drink whose day job involves working as executive officer at the Shetland Fishermen's Association. She is also one of the volunteer co-ordinators at the Shetland Christian Youth Camp which has taken place most summers for the last 25 years.The stunning location just above the West Voe beach at Sumburgh caters for groups of over 100 children and adults – and these wholesome wraps feature on the menu.

Makes 8

Pulled Pork

1.5kg pork shoulder – cut in half

1 tin tomatoes – 400g

1 teaspoon Dijon mustard

2 tablespoons runny honey

1 x 5cm piece cinnamon stick

½ nutmeg – grated

1 teaspoon allspice berries – crushed in a pestle and mortar

1 piece fresh ginger (15g approx) – cut into thin slices

2 cloves garlic – crushed and roughly chopped

1 level teaspoon salt

Wraps

100g plain flour

100g wholemeal flour

2 tablespoons olive oil

Large pinch salt

100ml warm water

Salad

Leaves, rocket, cucumber, lettuce, small sliced tomatoes – your choice.

Pulled Pork

1 Put all the ingredients except the pork into a pan and heat through, mixing well.

2 Place the pork pieces into the slow cooker, or a deep roasting tin, and add the sauce, mix around to coat.

3 Cook for 8 hours in a slow cooker or Rayburn, or 4-5 hours at 100°C in a conventional oven.

4 Lift the meat on to a plate or board and pull apart using two forks.

5 Remove the whole cinnamon and purée the marinade with a stick blender.

6 Transfer to a saucepan and thicken with a level teaspoon cornflour (or plain flour), blended with a little water.

7 Bring to the boil and stir until smooth and thickened.

Wraps

1 Mix all ingredients together and knead until smooth.

2 Divide into 8 pieces.

3 Roll each one into a circle.

4 Cook on a flat, dry pan over a medium heat until slightly browned and blistered.

5 Flip over and repeat on the other side.

6 Keep warm and soft under a clean tea towel.

To assemble

Spread a teaspoonful of the sauce over the wrap, then some pulled pork, then more sauce. Fold in the top and bottom, then the sides. Cut the wrap in half, at an angle, and off you go.

Slow-Cooked Spiced Whole Shoulder of Mutton

Mutton – the name given to an older sheep, has a more mature and full flavour which is particularly suited to long, slow methods of cooking. Most mutton sold for consumption will be 18 months or older but an 'auld yowe', three or four years old, will produce a truly memorable denner (dinner) and will be even more delicious when cooked on the bone, so a leg or shoulder is an ideal cut. Many Shetlanders have their own animals or know someone who does and will have plenty of denners in the freezer.

Serves 6

2kg approx shoulder of mutton on the bone

1 teaspoon salt

1 teaspoon allspice berries

3 cloves garlic peeled

50g piece fresh ginger

1 teaspoon whole cumin seeds

250ml water (or red wine if you prefer)

3 medium onions – peeled and thickly sliced

I have made a simple mixture of garlic, cumin, allspice and fresh ginger to rub into the meat and have added some thickly sliced onions around the joint to add flavour. Allow at least four hours slow cooking and a good half hour to rest the meat while you make gravy and get vegetables ready.

1   Preheat the oven to 220° C.

2   Make a rough paste with the salt, allspice, garlic, ginger and cumin in a pestle and mortar or blender.

3   Slash the skin of the mutton 3 or 4 times and rub the mixture all over.

4   Place the sliced onions into a roomy roasting tin and set the meat on top. Add the water or wine.

5   Cook for 20 minutes at full blast, then reduce the heat to 100°C and cook for a further 4-5 hours. (Overnight in the bottom of a Rayburn or equivalent solid fuel cooker would also do.)

6   Lift the cooked meat on to a warmed ashet.

7   I prefer not to make a thickened gravy in this case. Just skim off a bit of fat if necessary, add a glass or two of red wine or the water from cooking vegetables and bring up to the boil, simmer in the tin for 5 minutes, scraping off all the crispy bits.

8   Serve with a 'lang nev' (a good handful) of chopped parsley sprinkled over the meat.

➲ This is not haute cuisine – it is wholesome native meat full of flavour and with an insignificant number of food miles.

Reestit Mutton Pie

This recipe combines the famous and very special reestit mutton with a crisp, classic, homemade flaky pastry. You can, of course, use bought pastry, but do try this recipe for flaky pastry which makes a large batch that can be halved and frozen for another time, or maybe used for a tray of lovely sausage rolls. This recipe was first published in *Shetland Life* in January 2016 and has been extremely popular ever since.

Makes 4 individual hearty pies

Pastry

400g plain flour

150g butter – at room temperature

150g lard – at room temperature

150-175ml cold water

Good pinch of salt

Lemon juice – a good squeeze (the lemon juice helps the gluten to stretch which gives good flaky layers)

1 Prepare filling by cooking the vegetables in some reestit mutton stock for approximately 5 minutes. Then add the reestit mutton and a good handful of chopped parsley.

2 Sieve the flour and salt into a mixing bowl and rub in one quarter of the fat, until it is incorporated evenly.

3 Add the water and lemon juice and mix with a palette knife carefully, until an elastic but not sticky dough is formed. This will need a little judgement so don't add all the water at first. Knead very lightly.

4 Roll out to make a large rectangle with good square corners. Use a little flour, as necessary.

5 Cover the top two-thirds of the pastry with the second quarter of fat – evenly in small dots.

6 Fold into three by bringing the lower third (with no fat) up and the top third down.

7 You can now see how the pastry will become beautifully layered.

8 Press the pastry firmly with the rolling pin, both at the side edges and across the length. This will help to distribute air.

9 Give the pastry a quarter turn clockwise. Chill for at least half an hour.

10 Roll out, then repeat twice more so that all the fat is used up.

11 Do a final extra roll-and-fold, refrigerate again, then it is ready to use.

Continued overleaf

Reestit Mutton Pie (Continued)

Filling

350g carrots – cleaned
and diced

350g neeps – peeled
and diced

150g taaties – peeled
and diced

2 large onions –
roughly chopped

Freshly ground black pepper

A small bunch parsley
– roughly chopped

250g cooked reestit
mutton – cut into pieces

1   Prepare filling by part cooking the vegetables in some reestit mutton stock for approximately 5 minutes then add a good handful of chopped parsley along with the meat.

2   If you can, use a pie dish with a lip (a china pie dish is good and the traditional Falcon enamel dishes are easily available and are excellent).

3   Light the oven to 220°C – good and hot.

4   Roll out half the above quantity of pastry and use the pie dish to mark out and cut the lid to the correct size.

5   From the trimmings, cut a half-inch wide strip, moisten the lip dish with water and lay this round the dish. Make some pastry leaves or other decoration with the rest of the scraps – they are too good to waste.

6   Add the vegetables and mutton and use enough brö (stock) to keep the filling moist.

7   Carefully lift on the lid and use water to press it firmly on to the prepared edge. Flake up the edges using a sharp knife and make an attractive fluted edge with your thumb.

8   Add the pastry decorations and make a hole in the middle to help steam escape.

9   Beat a small egg and brush all over the top (but not the fluted sides as you want them to rise).

10   Place near the top of the oven on a baking sheet and bake initially for 20 minutes to get the top of the pastry a good golden brown.

11   Reduce the heat to 150°C and cook for a further 45-55 minutes. Lay a sheet of baking paper on top if it is browning too much.

12   Enjoy this fine pie with some lightly cooked Shetland kale or another green vegetable.

13   A glass of beer from the Lerwick Brewery would also go very well indeed.

Shetland Hand-raised Pork Pie

This is the homemade version of the classic, popular pie. Home-reared pork is widely available in Shetland and is delicious and full of flavour. If possible, do use fresh herbs and spices – the flavours will be far superior to dried or ready-ground. The hot-water crust pastry is not difficult but the finishing can be fiddly; my versions are certainly not things of beauty, but they taste great.

Makes 6 pies

Filling

500g pork shoulder – finely chopped or minced

250g pork belly – finely chopped or minced

150g lardons – or diced smoked bacon

1 onion – finely chopped

¾ teaspoon ground mace

¼ freshly grated nutmeg

1 teaspoon crushed fennel seeds (use a pestle and mortar if possible)

1 teaspoon juniper berries – roughly chopped with a sharp knife

1 tablespoon finely chopped sage

1 tablespoon finely shopped thyme

1 tablespoon finely chopped parsley

½ teaspoon salt and freshly ground black pepper

Pastry

500g plain white flour

1 teaspoon salt

150g lard

50g butter

200g water

Beaten egg to glaze

3 sheets gelatine

150ml chicken stock

1 Mix all filling ingredients thoroughly together and set aside while you make the pastry.

2 Sieve the flour and salt into a mixing bowl.

3 Put the lard, butter and water into a small pan and heat slowly, till the fats melt. Bring just up to boiling point.

4 Add to the flour and mix well with a wooden spoon. When cool enough, knead well on a lightly floured work surface till cool.

5 Preheat the oven to 180°C.

6 Divide the pastry into 6. Cut off about a quarter for the lids.

7 Roll out 6 circles and line 6 tins, or the outsides of 6 jars.

8 Pack the filling mixture into the pies and roll out the lids; using a little water to seal, pinch the edges well. Make a hole in the centre of the lid to allow steam to escape.

9 Brush the tops with beaten egg.

10 Cook for 30 minutes, then reduce heat to 150°C for a further 30 minutes. Leave until cold.

11 Finally, the jellied stock: soak the gelatine leaves in cold water for 5 minutes.

12 Heat the stock until boiling, add the gelatine and dissolve then allow to cool to room temperature.

13 Use a funnel to pour stock into the pies, a little at a time, for the traditional finish.

➲ You can make these free-standing by either hand-raising using a wooden mould or a jam jar or, alternatively, use a deep-holed large muffin tin.

Braised Shin of Beef

This is a very basic recipe but with outstanding flavour. I have used organic native Shetland beef from Jakob Eunson at Uradale Farm, which is across the voe from Scalloway. After being processed at the Lerwick abattoir, Jakob butchers his own animals which are sold locally. This cut is ideal for braising: the shin, or leg – bone in – requires long, slow, moist cooking and produces a wonderfully rich, gelatinous gravy which I have chosen not to thicken. It is even better the next day.

Serves 4

1 kg shin of beef (bone in) – ideally 4-5cm thick

1 tablespoon oil

1 large onion – diced

2 cloves garlic – crushed and finely chopped

150ml red wine

50ml passata (thick sieved tomatoes)

1 small bunch fresh thyme

2 bay leaves

Salt and freshly ground pepper

2 medium-sized carrots – in chunks

¼ medium-sized neep – in chunks

Parsley to serve

1   Preheat the oven to 125°C.

2   Brown the meat in the oil on both sides in a heavy casserole; lift out on to a plate.

3   Add the onion and garlic to the pot and allow to soften slowly. Add the wine, passata, seasonings and mix well.

4   Return to the pot and add a little water, if necessary, for the meat to be just covered.

5   Bring right up to the boil, then place in the centre of the oven.

6   Cook slowly for about 2 hours.

7   Add the carrot and neep, stir well and cook a further hour.

8   Add plenty of chopped parsley before serving.

9   Perfect with a big dish of 'shappit' taaties' (mashed potato) to absorb that delicious gravy.

Baking

aking is a matter of pride for many Shetlanders: it is about community, sharing, handing down recipes and skills and providing a welcome – almost always accompanied by a cup of tea. 'Tae and tabnabs' will involve (many) cups of tea accompanied by something sweet – at Up Helly Aa, weddings and all gatherings, especially where a bit of energy is required.

The 'Sunday Tea' is now famous even beyond Shetland: local community hall committees all over Shetland offer, for a modest charge, a range of scones, bannocks, sandwiches, cakes and biscuits to satisfy even the heartiest appetite. It is a very effective way of raising money for community or charitable causes, the baking is all donated and the hall committee members provide their time voluntarily. Roadside signs, social media and *The Shetland Times* will guide you to your destination.

Another popular way of sampling delicious home bakes is from one of the many cake fridges that can now be found all over Shetland. A cake fridge is basically a refrigerated display honesty box. Some are more seasonal but the range of produce is not limited to cake: they can include jam, bread, vegetables, eggs and there is also a dedicated mussels box near Aith. The original cake fridge established in 2019 is situated between Voe and Aith and now has a tea room next door in this beautiful scenic location.

Katja Stuebiger is a very creative baker and started making her unique and delicious range of German inspired cakes and savouries over 12 years ago, then in 2018 went on the road with her Unkenwagen selling delicious coffee too. She now operates the café with one of the best views in Shetland – at Sumburgh Head Lighthouse.

Bere and oats or 'aets' are the traditional Shetland-grown cereals and I really love using them whenever I can. Neither is grown commercially now – bere is imported from Orkney and oats mostly come from the Scottish mainland. Beremeal features in a number of these recipes and is the predominant ingredient in the bannocks while the oatmeal – of which there are four grades readily available locally – features in the soda bread, parkin and the oatcakes.

Many Shetlanders make their own bread either by machine or by hand and more so as the interest in artisan breads and sourdough increases. There are several bread recipes in *Shetland Food and Cooking* and a delicious soda bread recipe here.

There are currently five wholesale bakeries in Shetland, each with unique specialities, which supply retail shops all over Shetland six days a week.

The Sandwick bakery is over 100 years old; their traditional recipes for biscuits and bannocks in particular are those that were used when the bakery first opened. The Waas bakery makes a range of artisan breads including sourdoughs and a delicious 'tattie bread' made with Shetland potatoes. The Voe bakery is also over 100 years old and famous for its bannocks; it began life in 1915 at the request of the Navy to feed the sailors stationed nearby during World War One. Da Kitchen Bakery operates out of the Burravoe Hall in Yell. They are a smaller scale artisan bakery which specialises in cakes, breads and savouries using Shetland butter and dairy products. I have a particular weakness for their chocolate-dipped mini marzipan and chocolate sponges! The Skibhoul bakery in Unst makes a range of bread and traditional biscuits but their mini oatcakes made with sea water are particularly delicious.

There are also several new small businesses specialising in particularly delicious handmade cakes and patisserie; Scoop Wholefoods in Lerwick regularly stocks a great selection.

So, get your 'peenie' on – and start baking!

Oatmeal Stout Fruit Loaf

This delicious, moist, crumbly cake uses dried figs, dates and apricots as well as raisins and is a variation on a 'huffsie' or 'doofie' – a traditional Shetland fruit cake that is sometimes spread with butter. This version is a bit richer and more fruity; the fruit is soaked in 'Tushkar' – a lovely stout brewed by the Lerwick Brewery. The wholesomeness of this cake is also increased by the use of some oatmeal. This cake is high in fibre and natural sugars from the dried fruit. Use any combination of fruit to make up the 450g for the recipe. It will keep for several weeks if wrapped tightly in greaseproof paper and foil and it freezes well.

Makes up to 18 slices

200g butter – at room temperature

150g soft brown sugar

4 eggs – lightly beaten

250g self-raising flour

150g fine oatmeal

2 level teaspoons baking powder

2 level teaspoons cinnamon

450g dried fruit:
    100g apricots
    150g raisins
    150g figs
    50g dates

175ml 'Tushkar' stout (or similar dark stout) – if possible soak fruit overnight

1   Preheat the oven to 180°C and grease and line a large loaf tin – 26cm x 10cm – or two smaller ones. You could also make this in a 20cm round cake tin.

2   Sieve flour, oatmeal, cinnamon and baking powder on to a plate.

3   Cream butter and sugar until soft and add eggs.

4   Add soaked fruit and mix really well.

5   Add dry ingredients, mix very well; a good spatula is best for this job.

6   Put into the lined tin(s) and into the oven near the top.

7   Bake for 20 minutes at 180°C then reduce the heat to 150°C. You might need to lay a piece of baking paper or foil over the top to prevent over-browning

8   The cake will need about 1 hour in total. Cool in the tin and ideally keep for a day before eating.

Hot Cross Buns (or Not Cross Buns)

These buns are just too good to have only at Easter, so leave off the crosses if you wish. I have simplified the method and have used this version for many years, with inexperienced students, producing excellent results. The aroma in your kitchen will be amazing.

Makes 12

500g flour (a mixture of wholemeal and white gives the best results)

1 sachet easy blend yeast (7g)

50g butter – at room temperature

50g brown sugar

150g mixed peel

150g currants

2 large pinches salt

3 rounded teaspoons mixed spice

1 egg + warm water – totalling 300ml

1 egg for glazing

2 tablespoons runny honey

Crosses – make a paste as follows:

30g plain white flour

10g sunflower oil

10g cold water

Mix with a knife, roll out thinly and cut into 24 narrow strips.

1 Measure all the dry ingredients and the soft butter into a large bowl.

2 Crack the egg into a measuring jug and add warm water to give a total of 300ml .

3 Mix everything together.

4 Knead for a good 5 minutes until smooth and elastic – ideally in a mixer.

5 Put the dough into a bowl, cover and allow to rise for about 1½ hours at room temperature.

6 Turn out on to a lightly floured surface, knead for a minute, then divide into 12 pieces.

7 Shape into 12 buns and place on to a floured baking tray.

8 Prove (the second rise where the buns expand until nearly the finished size) for about ¾ to 1 hour, covered with a clean tea-towel.

9 Light the oven now – HOT! – 220°C

10 Make the crosses, if using.

11 Brush buns with beaten egg, put the crosses on top and bake for 15 minutes on a high shelf.

12 When done, brush with runny honey to give a sticky shine.

Sumburgh Lighthouse Chocolate Cake

This cake was commissioned by the late Angela Hunt – artist, textile designer, college lecturer and the driving force behind establishing the hugely popular café at Sumburgh Lighthouse – a much missed tour de force. She asked for two different wholesome cakes and this one and the Oatmeal Stout Loaf were what I concocted for her. They are both traditional family cakes and have proved extremely popular and straightforward to make. Not too rich, but enough chocolate to put a smile on your face. Ginger is a favourite spice for Shetland bakers. This tasty cake has crystallised stem ginger in the cake mixture, with ginger syrup and freshly-grated dark chocolate on the top.

Makes 8-12 slices

250g butter – must be soft
(at room temperature)

250g soft brown sugar

4 eggs

150g stem ginger –
chopped fairly finely

250g self-raising flour

2 level teaspoons baking powder

50g cocoa

100ml milk

To finish

2 tablespoons stem ginger syrup

25g dark chocolate – grated

1   Preheat oven to 180°C and line a round 8" (20cm) cake tin with baking paper.

2   Sieve flour, baking powder and cocoa on to a plate.

3   Cream butter and sugar until soft, then add the eggs, then ginger. Mix very well.

4   Add dry ingredients and the milk. Mix well with a spatula.

5   Transfer to the prepared tin and smooth the top with a palette knife.

6   Bake near the top of the oven for 20 minutes, then reduce heat to 150°C.

7   The cake will need about 1-1¼ hours in total. Lay a piece of baking over the top to prevent over-browning.

8   Allow to cool in the tin then transfer to a serving plate.

9   Before cutting, brush the top liberally with the ginger syrup and sprinkle a thick layer of grated chocolate over the top.

➔ Butter and milk come from Shetland Farm Dairies which is local and wholesome. Fresh eggs are widely available in numerous honesty boxes throughout Shetland as well at most local food shops.

Oatmeal Soda Bread

The absolute beauty of this wholesome bread is that (depending on how fast you are at weighing out the ingredients) you can probably have a loaf on the table from scratch in under an hour. It is even quicker to make than a batch of bannocks and uses buttermilk which Shetland Farm Dairies makes every week as a by-product of their butter production.

Makes 1 loaf

250g plain white flour

150g plain wholemeal flour

100g medium oatmeal

1 level teaspoon salt

1 rounded teaspoon baking soda

25g butter – at room temperature

500ml buttermilk

1 Preheat the oven to 200°C and place a baking sheet in the oven.

2 Have a sheet of baking paper ready.

3 Weigh all the dry ingredients into a large mixing bowl and rub in the butter.

4 Stir in the buttermilk and mix well. You should aim for a soft consistency.

5 Tip the dough on to the work surface, dusted with a little oatmeal.

6 Working quickly, shape into one round and place on to the baking paper.

7 Cut a deep cross into the top and transfer to the heated baking tray.

8 Bake for about 35 minutes until the loaf is risen and browned.

9 Allow to cook slightly before eating.

⊙ Soda bread is always best eaten when freshly made, spread with plenty of butter, to accompany soup, or as a sandwich with cheese, meat or other delicious fillings.

Cardamom Buns

These truly lovely fragrant buns really are a bit of a Scandinavian treat, made here with Shetland butter and milk. I make these a batch at a time and freeze them very successfully, then it's just five minutes in a warm oven to accompany a brew of good strong coffee. There is definitely a knack to the cutting and twisting of the dough and there are tutorials on Youtube to help, but it's the taste that's amazing, even if they are a bit 'ill shaepit' (misshapen) on your first attempt.

Makes 12

Basic Dough

500g strong white bread flour

7g dried instant yeast

Large pinch salt

50g butter

350ml milk – slightly
warmed in a pan

15 cardamom pods –
contents removed

50g caster sugar

1 level teaspoon cinnamon

Cardamom Butter Filling

150g caster sugar

150g unsalted butter at
room temperature

2 level teaspoons ground
cardamom (or cardamom seeds
crushed in a pestle and mortar)

To Finish

1 egg – beaten (egg wash for
glazing before cooking)

25g caster sugar, level teaspoon
ground cardamom and 50ml
water (for glaze after cooking)

1   Crack open the cardamom pods with a pestle and mortar, or use a knife, and add to the warm milk. Allow to infuse.

2   Weigh the flour, salt, cinnamon, yeast and sugar into a large mixing bowl, or use a stand mixer with a dough hook, and rub in the butter.

3   Strain the warm milk into the mixing bowl, discarding the pods.

4   Mix well for at least 5 minutes in the mixer or for 10 minutes by hand, until you have a smooth and soft dough.

5   Cover and leave for at least 2 hours to rise, or put in the fridge overnight.

6   Thoroughly mix together all the ingredients for the butter filling. Set aside at room temperature before using.

7   Line two baking trays with baking paper.

8   Briefly knead the dough and roll out thinly to form a 'landscape' rectangle measuring 35cm deep x 45cm wide.

9   Spread the cardamom butter all over, right to the edges. Mark lightly into three and fold the top third down and the bottom third up, giving three layers of butter/dough.

10   Cut into 12 equal strips, approximately 3.5cm x 11cm.

11   Cut each strip down the centre, leaving each attached at the top.

12   Twist each strip 2 or 3 times then tie the twist into a knot, tucking the ends underneath, and place each on a baking tray as you shape it.

13   Leave to rise for 45 minutes to 1 hour. Preheat the oven to 190°C.

14   Once they have doubled in size, brush gently with the egg wash.

15   Bake for 20-25 minutes until golden brown.

16   Meanwhile, prepare the sugar glaze: bring to the boil then allow to cool slightly.

17   When done, brush the syrup over the buns at least twice to give an amazing sticky shine.

Dark Beremeal Bannocks

Bere (Hordeum vulgare) is an ancient, six-rowed spring barley which dates back to the 8th century. It is no longer grown commercially in Shetland but it is in Orkney, where it is milled at the Barony Mills in Birsay. The flavour is slightly bitter and these plain bannocks are delicious with just butter, or with cold meat, e.g. salt beef, pastrami, Shetland lamb; with cheese, or as an accompaniment to a bowl of wholesome soup. They are equally good with a good spoonful of Shetland rhubarb jam. If you are unable to find beremeal, this recipe has been tested – and works very well – with rye flour instead. Plain yogurt can also be substituted for buttermilk.

Makes 12

200g beremeal

100g plain white flour

Large pinch salt

2 level teaspoons baking soda

1 level teaspoon cream of tartar

25g Shetland butter

300g Shetland buttermilk

1 Rub the butter into the sieved dry ingredients, add the buttermilk and mix to form a soft dough. Divide the mixture into three rounds. Flatten slightly to about 2cm thick.

2 Divide into quarters.

3 Cook on a medium-hot griddle or large flat pan for approx 5 minutes on each side. Cool in a tea-towel.

4 Bannocks freeze very well and are particularly good served slightly warmed with plenty of butter.

➲ In 2018 these bannocks, together with fine Shetland lamb, graced the London launch of Ann Cleeves's final book in her *Shetland* series – *Wild Fire* – and also at the popular Chiswick Book Festival.

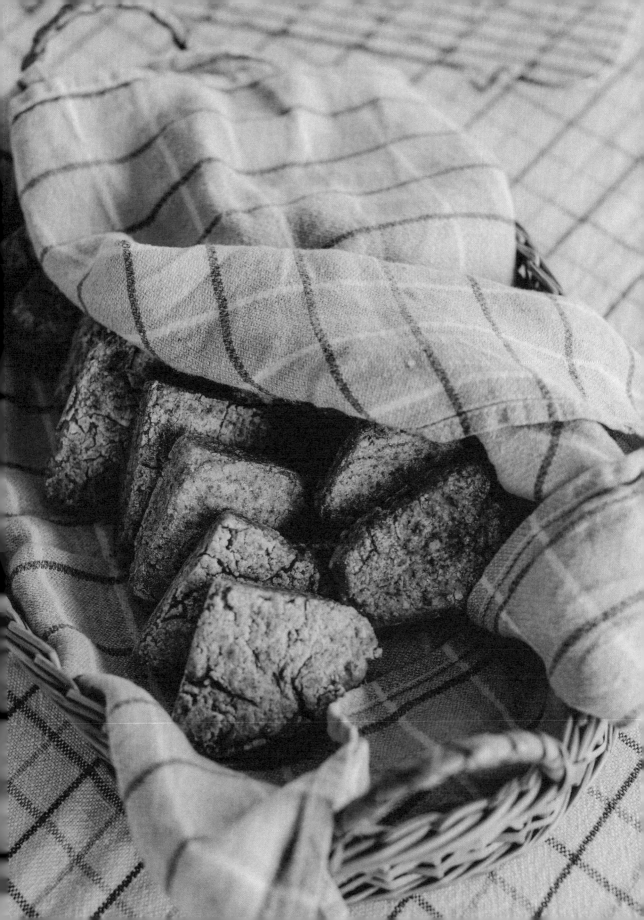

Beremeal Shortbread

Beremeal gives this shortbread a bit more body and depth of taste whilst still remaining light and crisp. Rye flour can be substituted if beremeal is not easily available.

Makes 12-18 small shortbreads

100g plain flour (or 75g plain: 25 semolina, for extra crunch)

50g beremeal (rye flour may be substituted)

100g unsalted butter (at room temperature)

50g caster sugar

1 Preheat the oven to 160°C.

2 Lightly mix the butter and sugar until soft, then stir in the flour.

3 Roll out thinly – ½ cm thick. Cut into squares or circles.

4 Bake for 20-30 minutes until pale golden. Cool on a wire rack – sprinkle lightly with caster sugar.

Spiced Treacle Bannocks

This is an updated recipe for Wilma Malcolmson's legendary treacle bannocks and this version is more treacly, fruity and spiced than her original. If you can grind the cloves in a pestle and mortar, and the nutmeg on a fine grater, the difference is really tremendous. Wilma was patron of Shetland Wool Week for the two pandemic years yet has seen her business grow and flourish in this time. Her talent, experience and skill in all aspects of the knitwear industry are hugely respected both in Shetland and around the world.

Makes 18

500g self-raising flour

2 level teaspoons baking powder

4 level teaspoons spice – ideally ground cloves, nutmeg, cinnamon, mixed spice

25g caster sugar (1 level tablespoon)

50g butter

150g raisins

100g treacle (about 4 dessert spoons)

1 egg

Half pint milk (285 ml)

1 Preheat the oven to 220°C.

2 In a small bowl, lightly beat the egg with about ¾ of the milk.

3 Sieve the flour, baking powder, spices and sugar into a large mixing bowl and rub in the butter.

4 Add the raisins.

5 Make a well in the centre and add the treacle and egg/milk mixture and mix with a knife.

6 Add more milk to make a soft consistency.

7 Roll out lightly to about 2cm thick.

8 Cut into triangles and bake in a hot oven for 15 minutes.

9 Cool under a tea-towel.

10 Eat warm, spread with Shetland butter.

The 'keps' (hats) in the photograph show the official colourways of the 2021 SWW hat, together with my late mother's maakin' belt (knitting belt) and some of Wilma's wires (needles).

Wilma's knitwear can be viewed and purchased at **www.shetlanddesigner.co.uk**

Also do look at **www.shetlandwoolweek.com**

Oatmeal Parkin

This is similar to a gingerbread and is very easy to make. The whisky can be left out if you prefer. Oatmeal makes it more nutritious and gives it a lovely, slightly gritty texture. It will improve and become more sticky after a day or two. You could also decorate with a little white icing and some pieces of chopped crystallised stem ginger if you need more sweetness.

Makes 16 pieces

100g butter

200g treacle

100g golden syrup

100g dark soft brown sugar

150g self-raising flour

150g fine oatmeal

1 rounded teaspoon baking soda

2 rounded teaspoons ground ginger

1 rounded teaspoon ground cinnamon

3 tablespoons milk

3 tablespoons whisky

1 egg – lightly beaten

1 Preheat the oven to 150°C. Line a 23cm square or round cake tin with baking paper.

2 Put the butter, treacle, syrup and sugar into a pan and melt slowly.

3 Sieve the flour, oatmeal, baking soda, ginger and cinnamon into a mixing bowl.

4 Add the slightly cooled liquid ingredients to the bowl, followed by the milk and whisky. Mix well.

5 Add the egg and transfer to the tin.

6 Bake in the centre of the oven for about 1 to 1½ hours. Cover with a sheet of paper if the top is browning too quickly.

7 Allow to cool and cut into squares – the next day, if possible.

If you need to keep your baking fresh do consider using wax wraps rather than single-use plastics. They are made here in Shetland too! Look for Kathryn's lovely designs at @shetlandwaxwraps on Facebook and Instagram.

Carrot Cake

This is my version of this classic cake. Shetland-grown carrots are as good as you'll get anywhere and the other ingredients are wholesome and delicious. It can easily be made in a deep, round cake tin but I have opted for a tray-bake tin here. Many recipes use oil instead of butter, which is fine, but I prefer the flavour of real butter. Maple syrup also adds a luxurious rich sweetness.

Makes 24 pieces

150g unsalted butter – soft and at room temperature

150g light soft brown sugar

200g carrots – coarsely grated

125g sultanas

125g dates – block dates are fine

50g dessicated coconut

175g walnuts – coarsely chopped

2 large oranges – rind and juice (keep some zest for decoration)

200g maple syrup

2 eggs – lightly beaten

275g flour – a mixture of 50:50 wholemeal and white is ideal

2 level teaspoons baking powder

1 level teaspoon ground cinnamon

½ level teaspoon freshly ground nutmeg

Icing

200g cream cheese

200g crème fraiche

2 tablespoons icing sugar – sieved

½ teaspoon vanilla essence

Grated orange rind – to decorate

1 Preheat the oven 190°C.

2 Line a tin measuring 32cm x 22cm with greaseproof paper.

3 In a large bowl beat together the butter and sugar until really soft.

4 Add the carrots, sultanas, dates, coconut, walnuts, orange, maple syrup and eggs and mix really well.

5 Sieve the flours, baking powder and spices on to a plate.

6 Mix everything very thoroughly and transfer to the prepared tin. Add 2 tablespoons milk if necessary to create a soft dropping consistency.

7 Bake near the top of the oven for about 40 minutes in total – reducing the heat after the first 15 minutes to 160°C.

8 Allow to cool in the tin.

9 Now make the icing: put the cream cheese, crème fraiche and vanilla in a mixing bowl, add the icing sugar and beat thoroughly.

10 Spread the icing over the cake, cut into squares and decorate with a little orange rind.

Acknowledgements

I am extremely grateful to many folk who willingly
provided advice and information for this book.
Thank you all for your time and help.

Ann Johnson	Johnny Simpson
Sheila Keith	James John Shearer
Hilary & Martin Burgess	John Martin Tulloch
Penny Thompson	Barbara Fraser
Margaret Roberts	Mary Andreas
Eric Graham	Jan Riise
Lauraine Manson	Kenny Pottinger
Gordon Johnson	Kushik Lala
Nicola Johnson	Anousha Cele
Sarah Thompson	Jay Joubert
Kirsten Williamson	Jakob Eunson
Katja Stuebiger	Johnny Sandison
Lesley Watt	Wilma Malcolmson
Tavish Scott	Hafsteinn Traustason
Leslie Anderson	David Polson

Specific thanks too, to Gilly Bridle for her patience and
skill with the adaptations to the clever cover design;
to Susan Molloy for being a joy to work with during the
photo shoots and for her stunning final selection of
photographs; and to Misa Hay for steering the project
skilfully and smoothly from start to finish.

To my family: Alexander, Deepa and Ayanda; Ruth,
William, Ivy and Magnus and Joseph.

Finally, a very special thank you to James.